El Salv

Peace on Trial

Contents

Published by Oxfam UK and Ireland
© Oxfam UK and Ireland 1997

A catalogue record for this publication
is available from the British Library.

ISBN 0 85598 361 2

Oxfam UK and Ireland

Rhodri Jones,/Oxfam

Kevin Murray

Ivan Montecinos

Mike Goldwater/Oxfam

The unfinished business of peace

At noon, on 16 January, 1992, representatives of the Farabundo Martí Liberation Front (FMLN), the Salvadoran government, and the United Nations sat around a U-shaped table in Chapultepec, Mexico, and signed a Peace Accord putting an end to twelve years of civil war in El Salvador. At that same moment, two hundred thousand Salvadorans, in San Salvador's Civic Plaza, waved red flags and joined together to sing *Sombrero Azul* (The Blue Hat), a song that had become the unofficial anthem of the insurgency. After such a painful and destructive war, an entire nation celebrated the coming of peace.

In his speech at Chapultepec, Salvadoran president Alfredo Cristiani spoke with startling frankness about the roots of the conflict. 'This painful and tragic crisis has political, economic, social, and cultural roots that are both old and deep. In the past, one of the pernicious characteristics of our national way of life was the absence of the mechanisms necessary to permit the free play of ideas... the absence of a truly democratic way of life.' The Chapultepec Accord sought to remove the military from political life and create new democratic institutions. Constructing a democracy would make it possible to pull up the 'deep and profound' socioeconomic roots of the conflict.

FMLN Commander Shafik Handal sounded a hopeful and conciliatory note in his speech. 'The FMLN enters peace opening the hand that used to be a fist and extending it in friendship to those against whom we have fought. This is as it should be in a disengagement without winners or losers.' Most of the cheering crowd in San Salvador that day shared those sentiments.

After the speeches and the songs, however, many of those gathered in the plaza returned home to a life of poverty that had worsened during the war. Their expectations were that the Peace Accord would mean a better life for themselves and their families.

United Nations negotiator, Alvaro de Soto, called the agreement a 'negotiated revolution'. He may have been rather overcome by the moment, but beyond question the signing of the Chapultepec Accord presented all Salvadorans with an historic opportunity.

What are the 'deep and profound' roots of the conflict hinted at by President Cristiani? How did the war, and then the peace, affect Salvadorans? And has the country been able to take that big step over the threshold at which the Peace Accord left them? Five years after the signing of the Peace Accord, it should be possible to give at least partial answers to these questions.

facing page, above
Celebration of the signing of the Chapultepec Peace Accords, San Salvador, 16 January 1992.

facing page, below
Slogans and bullet holes: emblems of the long-running war.

below Playing with toy soldiers was a reflection of everyday reality.

Jenny Matthews/Oxfam

The Land of Good Fortune

Bordered by Guatemala on the west and Honduras on the north and east, El Salvador appears on the map as a tiny sliver of land carved out of the coastal areas of those two nations. In the east, it reaches towards Nicaragua, with Honduras dividing the two with its tiny outlet to the Pacific at the Gulf of Fonseca. Just over 150 kilometres of spectacular, largely undeveloped Pacific coastline marks the country's southern boundary.

Three distinct geographical zones make up El Salvador: a narrow plain running along almost the entire Pacific coast; a volcanic range cutting a straight line through the country's heart; and an area of rugged, higher mountains just inside the northern border with Honduras. Because of the determinant historical role played by volcanic eruptions and earthquakes in this land of great seismic instability, the volcanoes dominate El Salvador's image of itself in literature and art.

With 5.4 million Salvadorans occupying its twenty-one thousand square kilometres, El Salvador is both the smallest and the most densely-populated country in the continental Americas. The civil war forced at least a million Salvadorans out of the country, and displaced much of the remaining population to the south and west. At the end of the war, two-thirds of the country's people lived in its south-west quadrant, including greater San Salvador.

The capital city sits in the Valley of Hammocks between three volcanoes. Coffee plantations, the primary source of El Salvador's wealth for the century and a half before the war, blanket large areas of the steep volcanic slopes. Only in the last 30 years has the coastal plain gained economic prominence as the government cleared land for cattle grazing and the cultivation of cotton and sugar cane. The northern mountains, always populated by poor farmers living at the margins of the nation's economic life, were the main battleground in the civil war.

One of Central America's largest rivers, the Lempa, crosses the country from north to south.

right
Map of El Salvador, to show principal towns and some of the places mentioned in this book.

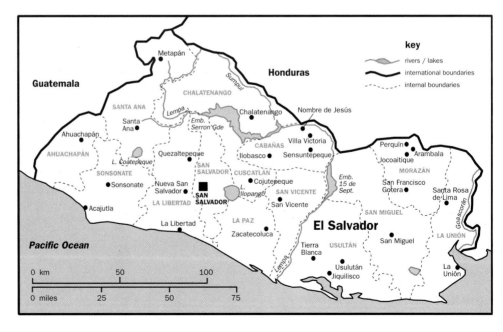

left Early morning, El Salvador.

below The destruction of two bridges crossing the Lempa struck a powerful psychological blow against a symbol of national unity.

The two large bridges built across the Lempa in this century served as the fragile connection between two regions divided by the great river. People from the eastern region, or *oriente*, maintain a distinct cultural identification, and that area is less developed in social and economic terms. When FMLN guerrillas blew up the two bridges crossing the Lempa in the early 1980s, it struck a powerful psychological blow against a symbol of national unity.

El Salvador's long border with Honduras has been the source of countless disputes that have turned the countries into traditional rivals. In 1969, that rivalry exploded into a shooting war. The International Court in The Hague resolved the border dispute by its 1992 decision ceding large pockets of the disputed land to Honduras. The situation of the few thousand of Salvadorans living in those mountainous areas remains a source of tension.

When the Spanish colonists arrived in 1524, dense tropical vegetation almost entirely covered the land then called Cuscatlán (The Land of Good Fortune), hampering the movements of the invasion force. Since that time, all but two per cent of that original forest cover has been stripped away. Today, the majority of El Salvador's forest consists of

an odd little tree brought to El Salvador from Africa via Europe: coffee.

During the rainy season from May to October, El Salvador seems verdant, almost lush. But by the end of the dry season in early May, El Salvador looks more like the marginal lands on the fringes of one of the world's great deserts than the tropical paradise described by the early conquerors from Spain. Deforestation, erosion, and diminishing water supplies have brought this once-flourishing land to the edge of an ecological disaster.

Are, then, the social and economic problems that led to the war simply a result

5

Rhodri Jones/Oxfam

Rhodri Jones/Oxfam

above, top Campesinos in Chalatenango. Rural culture has for centuries been based on the cultivation of corn.

above Church service in the Basilica del Sagrado Corazón, San Salvador. The priest is Monseñor Gregorio Rosa Chávez, Auxiliary Bishop.

AD. It appears that a massive eruption of the Ilopango volcano around 200 AD, caused a natural disaster from which this pre-classical society never recovered.

By 600 AD, a Mayan culture with strong ties to the great Mayan civilisation to the north became dominant on the western side of the Lempa. Mayan influence did not extend across the river, thus creating the cultural distinction that has been a recurrent theme in Salvadoran history. The complex Mayan culture was an agricultural society based on the cultivation of corn. The Mayans also made impressive mathematical and scientific advances on a par with contemporary civilisations in other areas of the world. For a variety of reasons, Mayan societies throughout Mesoamerica began to experience serious social and economic problems in the ninth century.

Over the next two centuries a new civilisation, linked by language and culture to the Aztec civilisation of Mexico, came to dominate the entire area between the Río Grande (now the border between Guatemala and El Salvador) and the Río Lempa, and had begun to extend its influence to the eastern side of the Lempa by the time the Spanish arrived on the scene. The indigenous Mexicans that accompanied the Spanish conquerors called its inhabitants *pipiles*, the hispanicized *nahuatl* word for children, because they spoke that language in a way that sounded child-like to the invaders.

In Cuscatlán the *pipiles* constructed an even more complex agricultural society than that of the Mayans, with a multi-layered class structure, cultivating a variety of crops and trading extensively. Their most important community — also called Cuscatlán — lived near the current site of San Salvador.

Although they employed irrigation along riverbanks, the *pipiles* used rudimentary slash and burn techniques for the cultivation of corn, beans, squash, and other crops. Since the gods of creation resided in corn, its planting, care, and harvest stood at the centre of their religious as well as economic life. The relation between the *pipiles* and their land took on a powerful spiritual significance.

Pipil communities held land in common under the control of the local leader, who

of the pressure of excess population on scarce natural resources? While population pressure on land, the country's most important natural resource, explains part of El Salvador's crisis, a full explanation requires an understanding of the distribution and use of natural resources through a long and troubled history.

In the Name of The Saviour

Little is known about the society based on hunting and gathering which flourished on the coastal plain and the volcanic foothills on both sides of the Lempa from about 1200 BC to 250 assigned land for family cultivation. Each family dedicated a certain amount of its produce to the priests and the temple, and slaves were forced to cultivate land for the warrior class. Some people, therefore, were supported by the production of others, but there was no concept of land being the private property of individuals.

As in the rest of the Americas, the arrival of the Spanish in Cuscatlán signalled social and cultural changes on an unprecedented scale. Hernán Cortéz, leader of the Spanish invasion of Mexico, sent one of his trusted lieutenants, Pedro de Alvarado, to take control of Cuscatlán and convert its inhabitants to Catholicism. He was accompanied by about 250 Spaniards and 5,000 Mexicans, members of indigenous groups that had allied themselves with Cortés.

The *pipiles* resisted fiercely. In the first battle with the invaders, the *pipil* leader Atlacatl sent an arrow through Alvarado's thigh, killing his horse and leaving the Spaniard with a permanent limp. Atlacatl's famous arrow would become an important symbol of resistance to injustice for future generations of Salvadorans.

Despite the experience and overwhelming superiority of arms of the Spaniards, it took them 15 years of repeated military campaigns to finally take control of Cuscatlán. In his diaries, Alvarado described the defenders' tactics of retreating into the mountains before his advance and resorting to ambush and other forms of warfare; tactics not unlike those of the rebels in the civil war almost five centuries later.[1] Similarly, Alvarado's brutal methods of suppressing indigenous dissent call to mind the 'scorched earth' policies involved in government efforts to pacify the Salvadoran countryside during the early 1980s. During the long struggle for control, the Spaniards renamed Cuscatlán after the Saviour, and established the colonial outpost of La Villa de San Salvador, which was abandoned and moved several times before it ended up on its present site.

Having secured their new prize, the victors quickly established a colonial administration

Jenny Matthews / Oxfam

left Bringing in the bean harvest.

Jenny Matthews / Oxfam

that would maximise the benefits accruing to both the Spanish crown and individual members of the conquering army. Since Cuscatlán had no mineral wealth, the new administration rewarded its soldiers with generous grants of the richest land being farmed by the *pipiles*. For the first time, land became private property. Some members of El Salvador's landed oligarchy trace their historical roots to these first acts of expropriation.

Even the best land, however, was valueless without labour to work it. Since very few of the *pipiles* would voluntarily work for the Spaniards, the colonial administration introduced a system of forced labour, or *encomiendas*. An *encomienda* put a certain number of indigenous people under the 'protection' of a Spanish landowner, and obliged them to work the land of their master.

The Spanish initiated the agroexport system that would dominate the national economy for centuries. They began a process of gradual dispossession of the indigenous population of its most sacred possession, the land. By 1770, fewer than 500 Spaniards controlled one-third of the country's land. Spanish traders exported cacao produced by indigenous farmers around Izalco and the balsam taken from trees closer to the coast, but El Salvador was never a major source of wealth for the Spanish Empire, in comparison with the mineral-rich countries of the south.

El Salvador's first landowners dedicated themselves to cattle-raising and the production of *añil*, the plant producing the prized blue dye indigo. This quickly became the region's leading export, but not without a price. The dye was extracted by indigenous labourers pressing the plants with their bare feet, and this was such a noxious process that before 1600 the Spanish authorities, concerned by reports of high numbers of deaths, outlawed forced labour in the production of indigo. Not surprisingly, the *hacendados* (Spanish landowners) ignored the law.

The historically unprecedented 'encounter between two worlds' had a devastating impact on the indigenous population. Anthropologists estimate that, between the years 1524 and 1551, the indigenous population of the land fell from 120,000 to 55,000. Epidemics caused by the introduction of new diseases caused more deaths than either military massacres or indigo production.

Indiodependencia and the 'golden bean'

By the early 1800s the colonial system had begun to break down, as the power of Spain weakened. The *criollos*, the Latin American-born descendants of the Spanish conquerors, had come to see control by Spain as an unnecessary burden and a brake on their own ambitions. An independence movement throughout Central America culminated in a regional declaration of independence from Spain in September 1821.

If anything, the situation of the poor majority became worse under *criollo* rule. In the new Republic of El Salvador only landowners of Spanish descent could expect full participation. In 1833, the Nonualcos, the indigenous groups living around the present sites of Zacatecoluca and San Vicente, rose up in protest at their mistreatment at the hands of the *criollos*. Nonualco leader Anastasio Aquino led the rebellion which captured the local garrison and might have taken control of the entire country. After the arrival of reinforcements, the *criollo* leadership sought to discourage future opposition by brutally putting down Aquino's rebellion and mounting the leader's head on a stake in the central plaza of San Vicente.

In the years following the Nonualco rebellion, a new export crop had begun to appear in El Salvador. As early as 1840, high-quality coffee was being profitably produced on the country's steep volcanic slopes. By 1864, the value of coffee production passed the declining income from indigo; the development of synthetic dyes in Europe lent even more urgency to the expansion of coffee production.

Despite over three centuries of encroach-ment by the hacienda system, large amounts of land still remained in the hands of indigenous communities, who raised corn, squash, and other food crops on small plots under communal control. For a government obsessed with the need to expand coffee production, such 'conservatism' represented an unacceptable obstacle to progress. In 1881 and 1882, the Salvadoran Legislative Assembly passed a series of laws abolishing the communal land-tenure system and establishing mechanisms for titling those lands to anyone who would use it for the cultivation of coffee and other export crops. Legal changes could not, however, end a way of life with roots thousands of years in the past. Regardless of legal decrees or the expanding market for coffee in the United States and Europe, Salvadoran campesinos would continue to search for land on which to plant their corn.

A system in need of guardians

Many of the investors who moved in to take advantage of the new land laws were fairly recent immigrants of European descent. With names like Hill, De Sola, Cristiani, Duke, Soundy, Dalton, and Llach, many of the dominant families of the Salvadoran coffee oligarchy trace their ascendancy to this period. The new coffee barons soon realised that simply abolishing communal lands would not ensure their profits from the potential coffee bonanza; the dispossessed campesinos had to be converted into a reliable, disciplined labour force.

Ana Cecilia Gonzalez /Oxfam

left Harvesting coffee on a co-operative plantation.

below The life-style of the rich in El Salvador is far removed from that of poor campesinos.

Mike Goldwater /Oxfam

On the heels of the land decrees came other laws governing day labour in agriculture, prohibiting organisation among rural workers, and creating an enforcement system of rural 'justices of the peace'. In 1889 the government created the first police forces in the coffee-growing areas, precursors of the infamous National Guard.

In 1931, the collapse of the world coffee market plunged the Salvadoran economy into crisis. The coffee oligarchy responded by drastically slashing the wages of workers.[2] Aided by the organisers of the newly-formed Communist Party of El Salvador — including one Farabundo Martí — coffee workers in the western part of the country organised protests against the wage cuts. The army used the unrest as a pretext to stage a coup d'état against the civilian government. Ill-planned and under-mined by spies among the communists, the insurrection among the coffee workers was crushed by government troops. Somewhere around 30,000 people were massacred in the next few days, the vast majority of them indigenous peasants. Salvadorans refer to the actions of those last days of January 1932 as *La Matanza* (*matanza* referring to a higher order of killing than a *massacre*).

The military authorities targeted campesinos wearing the traditional dress of the country's indigenous groups. Fearful of repression, people stopped wearing such clothing and suppressed other aspects of their culture. *La Matanza* was thus an important cause of the *mestización* — or assimilation of indigenous people to the point of cultural uniformity — of Salvadoran society. Army General Maximiliano Hernández Martínez moved quickly to consolidate his power and put into place economic reforms which, along with the wage cuts enforced by La Matanza, assured the survival of the coffee oligarchy. A half-century would pass before the next civilian president would take power in El Salvador.

right The military have long been a dominant force in Salvadoran society.

Mike Goldwater/Oxfam

The modernisation of misery

In the years after World War II, El Salvador's military rulers placed great emphasis on modernising the country's agroexport economy. Huge investments in infrastructure resulted in a new port facility at Acajutla, two massive hydroelectric dams along the Lempa, and a new coastal highway traversing the country from east to west. Manufacturing expanded rapidly through the dual strategies of import substitution and regional economic integration via the Central American Common Market (CACM).

However, the radically unequal foundations of Salvadoran society remained untouched by these changes, becoming if anything more extreme. Low wage rates and extraordinarily high rates of profit combined to replicate the earlier rural pattern of polarisation. Industrial investors relied on integration into a regional market, and made little effort to create a domestic market for manufactured goods.

The expansion of cotton and sugar cane production along the coastal plain and in the rich valleys between the volcanoes and the northern mountains concentrated land ownership into even fewer hands. According to one study, between 1892 and 1971 the average amount of land available to poor rural households declined from 7.4 to 0.4 hectares.[3] But it was not simply that there were too many Salvadorans on the land: 85 per cent of the decline was due to increasing concentration of land ownership and only 15 per cent to population increase.

As many as 300,000 Salvadoran campesinos responded to the lack of land by crossing the border into Honduras, where land was relatively plentiful. The 1969 Soccer War — so named because it was touched off by a fight in a soccer game between the two nations — forced the return of nearly all of those families. By the late 1970s, 40 per cent of rural Salvadoran families

Rhodri Jones/Oxfam

were without land, thereby creating a social emergency in the countryside. According to The United States Agency for International Development (USAID), over 80 per cent of the rural population lived below the government-defined poverty line, and three in four children under five years of age showed signs of malnutrition.

Ironically, during the period 1960–79, macroeconomic indices showed a country enjoying high rates of economic growth. Such statistics revealed little about the lives of poor Salvadorans, especially in the countryside where a pressure cooker heated by injustice once again reached the point of explosion.

above Searching rubbish dumps for items to recycle provides a precarious livelihood.

The impossible war

Despite the desperate poverty of so many of its people, El Salvador of the early 1970s seemed an unlikely place for a guerrilla war. The memory of *La Matanza* still haunted potential rebels and the defeats of several Latin American revolutionary movements had left a small, conservative Salvadoran Communist Party (PCS) even more reluctant to revolt. When a near-sighted union activist from San Salvador named Salvador Cayetano Carpio led a small group of radicals out of the PCS to form the Forces of Popular Liberation (FPL), few people outside of military intelligence paid much attention. The military still ruled El Salvador with an iron hand.

Urban opposition movements of workers and students existed in some form throughout the period of military rule. An upsurge in that opposition gained support within the military and toppled Gral, Maximiliano Hernández Martínez in 1944, but did not achieve lasting civilian rule. In the countryside, where labour organisation was illegal and the military exerted its greatest influence, campesinos had fewer ways to express dissent or demand better living conditions. The efforts, during the 1960s, of groups close to the Roman Catholic church and the Christian Democratic Party to organise agricultural co-operatives into the Salvadoran Federation of Christian Agricultural Co-operatives (FECCAS) represented the first significant rural organising in more than three decades.

Many factors turned the nascent social movements of the 1960s into the torrent of opposition that, by the late 1970s, threatened to bring down the military government of General Carlos Humberto Romero. The worsening social crisis pushed many Salvadorans to organise as an act of desperation. In massive electoral frauds in 1972 and 1977, the military overruled national elections clearly won by a broad opposition movement of workers, students, professionals, and organised peasants anchored in the Christian Democratic Party. These 'stolen' elections convinced thousands more Salvadorans of the impossibility of peaceful change.

Mike Goldwater/Oxfam

Ana Cecilia Gonzalez/Oxfam

Dramatic changes were meanwhile taking place within the Roman Catholic Church. Traditionally an extremely conservative institution at the service of the oligarchy, in the wake of the Second Vatican Council the church began to take seriously the call for a 'preferential option for the poor'. This shift in allegiance transformed the social landscape throughout Latin America. In El Salvador, no understanding of the growth of a mass opposition is possible without reference to the pivotal role of the 'popular' church.

Armed with a new, socially-progressive reading of the Bible, many young priests and nuns began to organise small groups for study and reflection in their congregations. These 'Christian Base Communities' multiplied rapidly and became the basis of a sustained demand for better living conditions. Once people decided that life need not be a time of suffering in anticipation of salvation after death, they became capable of previously unthinkable acts of defiance.[4] The Salvadoran army knew only one response to such insolence — brutal repression. But now, repression only served to harden resolve. Popular organisations grew quickly in the capital and the countryside despite increased killings and disappearances.

Moved by what he saw as the injustice of the military's response to the cry of the people, Archbishop Oscar Arnulfo Romero of San Salvador underwent his own transformation and became a national voice for the rights of the poor.[5] Salvadorans remember the late 1970s as a time when one could walk through rural hamlets on a Sunday morning without missing a word of Romero's homily. Every house had its radio tuned in to 'Monseñor'.

Cayetano Carpio and his fellow revolutionaries were not idle. In addition to the FPL, the Guerrilla Army of the Poor (ERP), the National Resistance (RN), and the Central American Revolutionary Party (PRTC) all emerged in the first half of the 1970s. They gained members as repression and electoral fraud radicalised the popular movements; and developed the capacity to carry out increasingly sophisticated armed actions throughout the country.

Mike Goldwater/Oxfam

above Demonstration to mark the fourth anniversary of the assassination of Archbishop Romero.

Hope for a peaceful resolution to the conflict flickered briefly in October 1979, when a group of young army officers engineered a coup that promised to end military rule and initiate a transition to democracy. The victorious plotters put in place a five-person civilian-military junta to lead the country until elections, promising democratisation and structural reform of the economy. The extreme right responded with a spate of murders and disappearances. The spiral of violence presented the junta with a painful dilemma over how long to continue legitimising the repression by their presence. By the time of Monseñor Romero's assassination on 24 March, 1980, the first junta had completely dissolved. This opened the way for a group of opportunistic politicians committed to pressing forward with formal democratisation regardless of the degree of brutality that lay beneath it. Napoleón Duarte, a Christian Democrat robbed of the presidency by fraud in 1972, joined the second ruling junta on the eve of the Romero assassination and quickly became its leading figure and the rock upon which the United States constructed its El Salvador policy for most of the next decade. Mutilated corpses began to appear at the side of the road with increasing frequency, as the death squads operated with complete impunity. One source estimates total political murders at 5000 for 1980 and double that in 1981. Most surviving activists either left the

facing page, above May 1986. Soldiers carry out an exercise in a village, breaking an agreement to respect its neutrality.

facing page, below Army patrol in a village. The war deepened the divisions in El Salvadoran society.

above Simple memorials to some of the 1,000 unarmed civilians massacred at El Mozote, Morazán, in 1981.

Larry Boyd/Oxfam

country or joined the FMLN in the mountains. Against this backdrop, the revolutionaries called for an insurrection to topple the government. In late 1980, they formed the Farabundo Martí Front for National Liberation (FMLN), and launched the 'final offensive' in January 1981. This marked the beginning of a full-scale civil war: a 'total' war that would dominate national affairs until early 1992.

The impact of the civil war on this tiny country almost defies analysis. Of the 80,000 people who died, at least half were civilians murdered by the army, the security forces, and para-military death squads because of their presumed connections to the guerrilla movement. At least 70,000 others were seriously incapacitated by a war-related injury.

The fighting displaced one million Salvadorans (a fifth of the total population) from their homes. The diaspora sent Salvadorans all over the world, with many ending up in the United States, most without immigration documentation.

As is often the case in civil wars, the extreme social polarisation of the war in El Salvador divided every rural village and urban neighbourhood, every institution of civil society, and even divided families. The suffering resulting from the war spared no family and left many in ruins with some members dead and the rest scattered over

the land like seeds carried by the wind. What measure fully expresses the impact of such a war on a society built on kinship ties within and between extended families?

The United States buys a stalemate

In the early stages of the war, the guerrillas clearly held the upper hand, with major military victories and dramatic acts of sabotage. In a variant of the classic pattern of guerrilla warfare, instead of remote rural bases, the FMLN substituted widespread popular support; the guerrilla mantra 'The people are our mountains' only slightly exaggerated the real situation.

The corruption and incompetence of the Salvadoran Armed Forces (ESAF) played into the guerrillas' hands. Already the dominant force in Salvadoran society, the army grew greatly in size and influence during the war. At its peak in the late 1980s, the army numbered at least 60,000 members, the vast majority of them poor, uneducated peasants. Most young recruits entered the army via a forced recruitment process that bordered on kidnapping. Once in, they were subjected to a programme of physical and ideological abuse that either broke them completely or prepared them to do absolutely anything to defend their country against 'Communist subversion'.

Trained to repress unarmed civilians, the ESAF proved much less effective against a clever, highly-motivated guerilla movement. In the early years of the war, the army pursued a 'scorched earth' approach to clear the civilian population from areas of guerrilla activity. These operations resulted in numerous massacres — such as the one at El Mozote, Morazán in December 1981 in which as many as one thousand civilians were summarily executed — but they did not defeat the FMLN.

Fearing the fall of the government and its replacement by an unfriendly pro-Communist regime similar to the Sandinistas in Nicaragua, the United States began to rush aid and advisors to the ESAF. For Ronald Reagan, El Salvador became the place to draw a 'line in the sand' in Central America. During the 12 years of war, US aid to this tiny country amounted to $6 billion.[6] On a per capita basis, only Egypt and Israel received more US aid during this period.

While the massive intervention in the civil war represented qualitatively new levels of participation in Salvadoran affairs, the US had exerted a powerful influence for nearly a century. Since the late nineteenth century, US companies had battled the British for control of rail and maritime transport, banking, and other strategic industries in El Salvador and the rest of Central America. The plan to open a canal through Nicaragua made the Gulf of Fonseca a primary strategic concern, and, as El Salvador's leading coffee customer, the United States had considerable leverage. By the 1960s, when the Alliance for Progress projected a broadened role for US economic aid throughout Latin America, Salvadorans recognised the veto power of *La Embajada* (the US Embassy) over the country's internal affairs.

US aid succeeded in propping up the government, but could only create a military stalemate in which the FMLN operated freely in large areas of the countryside, and maintained urban commando groups in San Salvador. While the existence of a degree of military balance was obvious to even the casual observer at the end of the 1980s, the Salvadoran military and many of its US advisors insisted that the guerrillas had been reduced to decentralised bands with very limited military capacity.

The guerrilla offensive of November 1989 demonstrated the absurdity of such assertions, while also showing the limits of the guerrillas' popular support. Thousands of FMLN fighters launched simultaneous attacks on over 100 military targets throughout the country. The rebels actually took and held large areas of the capital for several days, but the level of repression prevented the civilian insurrection the FMLN had hoped for. The superior firepower of ESAF forced the guerrillas to withdraw, leaving behind unprecedented destruction and hundreds of dead.

During those same fateful days, the murder of six Jesuit priests, their housekeeper, and her daughter demonstrated the moral bankruptcy of the US government's claim that a professionalised Salvadoran army had become a force for democratisation. The US decided to cut its losses and support a negotiated peace. For very different reasons, the leaders of the FMLN, a war-weary civilian population, and many members of the Salvadoran economic elite drew the same conclusion, and peace crept onto the national agenda.

left Demonstration on the first anniversary of the assassination of the six Jesuit priests, their housekeeper and her daughter.

Jenny Matthews/Oxfam

Miriam's story

Miriam Chicas grew up in Perquín, the largest town in the northern region of the department of Morazán.

❛ It wasn't a very developed town. Most of the wealth was in the hands of two or three families, with the rest living in poverty. I came from a family of 14 children. We were very poor, but my parents knew how to raise us.

The people around Perquín have always survived from wood-cutting and coffee. There has always been exploitation around here, but I, of course, didn't understand it then.

When the war began, most of us here in town didn't understand what was going on. I remember that in 1978 my father lent the cart to some cousins who wanted to haul some corn. They brought the cart back printed with the letters 'LP–28' for the Popular Leagues – 28 February. Armed groups had begun to operate in the region. Our family still believed in the goodness of the National Guard, that they took care of the people and all that.

The repression came soon after that. Beginning in 1979, there were captures almost every day; they brought back all these prisoners. We began to wonder why all these people were being brought into town.

I worked in City Hall for a year and would hear the cries of the people being tortured. But I still didn't understand why, although I heard people say that the prisoners were from the Frente.

As the guerrillas became more active, things got worse in Perquín. Families were divided, and many people left. Some of us stayed, but in constant fear. In 1981, the Frente took Perquín for the first time, for four days. We were afraid at first, but we calmed down as we saw people we knew among the guerrillas: people from other towns, friends of ours.

After that came a long period of time where the army would control the town for a while, then the guerrillas would come back. Often the bombardments and shooting would be so bad that we'd have to leave town for a few days.

Why did we stay? No, we weren't supporters of the guerrillas, and we didn't get used to that sort of life. We stayed because we saw that the war was all over the country. We'd have to face it one way or another wherever we were. We had to be some place: why not stay in the place we knew?

We finally left in 1984. We crossed into Honduras and ended up with 500 others in a camp near Colomoncagua. I was given work in health and they put my husband, Oscar, in charge of food distribution. Since this was our first experience of collective work, we were hesitant, but we adapted quickly. Life was hard, but good. What one didn't have, somebody else had: we exchanged, we borrowed, we shared. Everything was collective except our kitchens. Each of us had our own stove.

When we came back to Perquín eight months later we had a very different vision. We began to work in community organisations. Oscar became a member of the community council and I started to work through the church. We women hadn't been very active outside of our homes, but we began to sense the need to do something. Many of us came to that commitment out of our faith.

I remember when we women took off after the soldiers that had captured a large group of men and women for the crime of participating in an administrative training given by the guerrillas. We brought back some of the prisoners, but not all of them. These were very powerful experiences for us, our first activities as the Congregation of Mothers.

The military blockade wouldn't allow even a pound of sugar into northern Morazán. We women first broke that blockade in 1987 when we asked the Archdiocese for food. They approved a six-month supply of food, but to get it we had to get a pass from the military garrison. Imagine! We had to go into the garrison and talk to the colonel. Then we had to get the food back here, with no bridge over the Torola River. It was worth it because it really helped people. It also helped me realise how organisation can give us strength.

We haven't lost the vision that only by organising can we hope to overcome our problems. The Peace Accords stopped the bullets and the bombs, but many of the problems that started the war are still with us. Maybe they aren't as bad as before the war, but things haven't advanced as much as they sometimes say. There are still many difficulties and many things to resolve in this community. ❜

In April 1994, the people of Perquín elected Miriam mayor. She was the only woman among the 15 FMLN mayors elected at that time. Subsequent divisions in the FMLN left her party affiliation uncertain, and probably cost her the 1997 election, which she narrowly lost to the ARENA candidate.

Carmen and Chica:
A testimony of suffering, faith, and action

Personal testimony of suffering became a powerful weapon for church activists in El Salvador. Today, almost two decades after the periods of the worst repression, Salvadorans continue to share such stories as a way of never forgetting. On a trip to the United States in 1996, Carmen, a woman with long experience in the base community movement, told the story of one of the great moments of revelation in her life.

❛ I was working in a rural community, sometime in 1982, at the height of the government repression. This particular family was deeply involved in the work of the church: parents, children, extended family, working as catechists, Delegates of the Word, maintaining the work of the church among the people. It was not an easy time to be doing this work, but they were so strong and determined.

One evening armed men came to the house, in uniforms, from one of the military brigades. They told everyone to lie face down on the floor. They said that if anyone dared to raise their heads they would be blown away. Then they took two of the daughters in the family, Zenaida who was 15 and Cecilia who was 25. They dragged them away as the family lay waiting in terror. The next morning their mother, Paula, asked me to accompany her to look for her daughters at the military posts. We went to the barracks of several different military companies, we went to the Treasury Policy, the National Guard. No one admitted to having them. No one knew where they were.

After weeks of searching, their bodies finally turned up. Their breasts had been cut off. Their eyes had been pulled out of their sockets. There were signs of torture all over their mutilated bodies. They had been raped and finally, mercifully, they had been shot.

What happened next is one of the most powerful experiences I have ever had. That mother knelt down beside the bodies of her two mutilated daughters and she asked the God of Life to forgive those who had done this to her children. And she prayed that they might one day repent of the evil they had done. ❜

Speaking after Carmen's story, her friend, Chica, drew the link between faith and action that gave the base community movement its resilience.

Mike Goldwater/Oxfam

above March 1984. Living in constant fear of attack became part of everyday existence for peasant families.

right Worshipper at a Roman Catholic service.

Rhodri Jones/Oxfam

❛ Being a Christian base community is not simply about praying the Rosary and going to Mass. It is about action. As we reflect on the work of God, we are called to act as a body. Because if we do not build the Reign of God here on earth, there will be nothing for us in the hereafter.[7] ❜

Ana Cecilia Gonzalez/Oxfam

Mike Goldwater/Oxfam

Ana Cecilia Gonzalez/Oxfam

Jenny Matthews/Oxfam

Civil war in El Salvador:
a chronology

1970 Formation of Popular Forces of Liberation, first guerrilla group advocating armed revolution.

1972 Fraudulent election robs opposition of victory over military-supported candidates. Revolt of young army officers put down; opposition presidential candidate Napoleón Duarte arrested, tortured, and exiled.

1975 Military kills dozens at demonstration by university students; general radicalisation of student movement.

1977 Monseñor Oscar Arnulfo Romero named Roman Catholic Archbishop of San Salvador.

Rutilio Grande, Jesuit priest working with poor peasants north of San Salvador, murdered by right-wing death squads.

Col. Humberto Romero elected president in a second fraudulent election. Bloody reprisals against opposition after elections.

Catholic Church boycotts inauguration.

1979 Escalating violence; US-supported coup by young officers promises an end to military rule and broad reforms.

Ronald Reagan elected President of the United States on a platform of 'rolling back' communism, especially in Latin America.

1980 Repression worsens. Monseñor Romero assassinated while saying Mass in San Salvador.

Farabundo Marti Liberation Front (FMLN) formed to coordinate uprising by armed revolutionary groups.

Entire leadership of above-ground Democratic Revolution Front (FDR) kidnapped from Jesuit high school in San Salvador and murdered.

Four US churchwomen kidnapped, raped and murdered.

1981 FMLN launches 'final offensive', which fails, but leads to generalised guerrilla war.

Death squads kill thousands across country. Activists either leave country or go underground.

Ultra-nationalist ARENA party formed under leadership of Major Roberto D'Aubuisson.

War intensifies; military undertakes 'scorched earth' campaigns against civilian supporters of guerillas. Thousands killed or displaced. Military massacres over 1000 unarmed civilians at El Mozote, Morazán.

1984 US-supported alternative to D'Aubuisson and ARENA, Napoleón Duarte, elected president on the Christian Democratic party ticket; initiates peace talks. Opposition from military and hard-line posture from guerrillas; talks fail.

1985 Underground since 1980, Salvadoran popular movement reappears to organise opposition to Duarte government.

1986 Earthquake in San Salvador worsens already desperate conditions of war-displaced population.

1987 Regional peace initiatives under leadership of Costa Rican President Oscar Arias begin to show results. Esquipulas II Peace Accord commits Central American governments to the search for peace.

1988 Catholic Church initiates National Debate for Peace with over 60 participating organisations.

George Bush replaces Ronald Reagan as US President.

1989 FMLN makes conditional offer to participate in elections. Government refuses offer.

ARENA candidate Alfredo Cristiani wins presidential elections, agrees to negotiations with FMLN.

Bombing of FENASTRAS trade union headquarters; FMLN withdraws from negotiations, launches military offensive, attacking range of targets throughout country. US-trained elite army unit enters Central American University and murders six Jesuit priests, their housekeeper, and her daughter.

1990 Government and FMLN resume negotiations with UN mediation.

Caracas agreement signed, setting agenda for a negotiated solution to conflict.

Partial agreement signed in San José, Costa Rica formalising human rights guarantees and UN monitoring role.

1991 Legislative elections: first left-wing opposition parties in Legislative Assembly. Second and third partial agreements remove final barriers to peace.

UN monitoring mission (ONUSAL) in San Salvador and other cities. President Cristiani and FMLN agree on general outlines of Peace Accord.

1992 Peace Accord signed, 16 January, Chapultepec, Mexico, with effect from 1 February.

facing page, top to bottom

• Protest march after the arrest of four members of a co-operative.

• Army on patrol.

• Woman at an anti-government demonstration.

• The Town Hall at Perquín, destroyed during the war.

right, top to bottom

• Member of the 1st brigade, Mariona.

• Peace demonstration, 1991.

• Funeral of a campesino.

• Mural on the campus of the National University in San Salvador.

Rhodri Jones/Oxfam

Rhodri Jones/Oxfam

Mike Goldwater/Oxfam

Rhodri Jones/Oxfam

19

¡GANAMOS LA PAZ!

When the sun rose from behind the San Vicente volcano at dawn on 1 January, 1992, San Salvador stood unusually silent. After a long, hard night of celebrating, few residents had emerged from their homes. Not everyone had been sleeping: on what seemed like every other street corner, supporters of the FMLN had painted, in large, red block letters, ¡GANAMOS LA PAZ! (We Won the Peace).

During the very last minutes of 1991, President Alfredo Cristiani and the FMLN's General Command had signed an agreement which would lead, two weeks later, to the signing of a formal Peace Accord in Chapultepec, Mexico.

There had been many obstacles on the bumpy road to Chapultepec. A small group of public figures — including Arturo Rivera Damas, Romero's successor as Archbishop, and Jesuit leader Ignacio Ellacuría — had spoken out in favour of a negotiated solution to the conflict.[8] For the Salvadoran right, however, any talk of negotiations with the 'terrorists' of the FMLN amounted to treason. Despite the risks involved, the demands for peace grew stronger, especially from within the Salvadoran churches.

Christian Democratic President Napoleón Duarte orchestrated dramatic dialogue sessions with the FMLN in the mid-1980s,

below Rally to support the peace talks in 1990.

Jenny Matthews/Oxfam

but his initiative was more show than substance. At one point, Duarte stood near the town of La Palma, Chalatenango and shouted over a loudspeaker for the guerrillas to come down from the hills and talk.

In 1988, the Catholic Archdiocese convened dozens of popular organisations to form the Permanent Committee for the National Debate for Peace (CPDN), and organised regular mobilisations calling for the government to negotiate peace. To the surprise of many observers, the right-wing ARENA government sought negotiations with the FMLN soon after taking power in June 1989, but neither side was ready to gamble everything on peace, and the talks failed.

In the aftermath of the November offensive, the government and the FMLN returned to the negotiating table in early 1990 with renewed seriousness. They agreed to include a new player in the peace process: The United Nations. Other international actors helped the momentum toward peace. Colombia, Mexico and Venezuela formed a group of Friends of the Secretary General and mobilised diplomatic support for the negotiations throughout Latin America; the European Union spoke with one voice in favour of peace; and the Bush administration even dispatched its Under-Secretary of State, Bernard Aronson, at several key moments to 'encourage flexibility' among Salvadoran government and military leaders. Secretary-General Javier Pérez de Cuéllar intervened personally in the talks and invited the parties to the UN in New York to complete the agreement. In the waning moments of 1991, as the self-imposed deadline for the negotiations approached, the President and the FMLN signed the protocol leading to the end of the armed conflict.

The Salvadoran Peace Accord

While the Peace Accord signed at Chapultepec Park in Mexico City on January 16, 1992 was the crowning achievement of the peace process, earlier agreements had laid some of the foundations.

The Caracas Agreement, May 1990: set the agenda and ground rules for peace talks, and established the critical role of the UN.

Rhodri Jones/Oxfam

above Singing for peace, 1991.

The San José Human Rights Agreement, June 1990: established a mutual commitment to respect for human rights even as the war continued. Gave the task of monitoring compliance to a UN commission (ONUSAL).

The Mexico Agreement, April 1991: detailed constitutional amendments related to the Armed Forces, the judicial system, and the electoral system just in time for the outgoing Legislative Assembly to vote on them. Planned the establishment of a Truth Commission to investigate human rights violations during the war.

The New York Agreement, September 1991: set aside percentage of places in the new National Civilian Police for ex-combatants of the FMLN. In return, the Frente withdrew its demand that its units be integrated directly into the Armed Forces. Established The National Peace Commission (COPAZ), a multi-party body to co-ordinate supervision of the implementation of all peace agreements.

The Declaration of New York, December 1991: With time running out on the term of UN Secretary General Javier Pérez de Cuéllar, the government and the FMLN made a dramatic declaration just before midnight on New Year's Eve, calling for the signing of an agreement on 16 January 1992 and a cease-fire as of 1 February. [9]

The Chapultepec Accord, January 1992:

This historic document finalised all the partial understandings reached in the previous agreements and incorporated the results of the last three months' of negotiations. History will most likely remember the accord for ending the guerrilla war and altering the relationship between the military and society, but it also included important agreements in many other areas.

Demilitarisation: size of the military reduced by half; worst human rights violators purged from Armed Forces officer corps; functions of army constitutionally limited to national defence; public security removed from military control and placed in the hands of a newly-created National Civilian Police; military 'doctrine' altered to reflect civilian control of society.

Justice System: system professionalised and de-politicised through creation of new process for election of Supreme Court justices and overseeing the work of local judges; constitution amended to streamline the legal process and assure the rights of those accused of crimes; new institution, the Office of the Human Rights Ombudsman, created as a quasi-governmental monitor of respect for human rights throughout society.

Electoral System: accords speak of the need to redesign the entire electoral system (registration, voting, campaigning, vote-counting) to make it more accessible and democratic, and to guarantee the rights of the FMLN and other opposition parties, but the specific changes are much less significant: a new, less partisan Supreme Electoral Tribunal formed to oversee the process and guarantee the fairness of all elections.

Economic System: relatively little advance in this area: government and FMLN agreed to make further changes as necessary through new democratic system; government committed to carry out a National Reconstruction Plan to integrate the ex-combatants of both sides into the national economy, to repair social infrastructure destroyed by the war, and to rehabilitate the economies of the ex-conflictive zones; land would be transferred to about 40,000 ex-combatants of both sides and civilian supporters of the FMLN; a Socioeconomic Forum set-up to promote discussion of economic problems among all sectors of society.[10]

All participants realised that the implementation of the Peace Accord would be at least as difficult as its negotiation. While both sides committed themselves to specific actions, much of the responsibility for the actual implementation lay with legislators and governmental officials. Steps had to be taken quickly to establish good faith, before the FMLN demobilised its troops, but many of the most critical actions would not take place until after the FMLN had destroyed its most powerful bargaining chip, its arms. In that sense, the FMLN made something of a leap of faith, trusting that international pressure and the determination of the Salvadoran people would make up for any lack of political will on the part of the government to carry out its side of the bargain.

One FMLN leader summarised the danger by saying, 'We're paying for this house before the walls are even finished. We'll need lots of help to make sure the job gets done.' He was referring to the need for the Salvadoran public to demand full compliance, but also to the important role of international verification, especially that carried out by the UN verification mission, ONUSAL.

ONUSAL: The need for a good example

The UN entered the Salvadoran peace process in early 1990 when both sides agreed to solicit the 'good offices' of Secretary-General in the search for peace. Under the leadership of Alvaro de Soto, the UN team quickly assumed the role of mediator in the talks. They urged both sides to clarify positions, made proposals to resolve sticky issues, and pushed for partial agreements along the way to keep the process going.

There has been some criticism of the UN's tactics; for example, that the failure to involve UN economists to consider resource needs during the demobilisation worsened post-war dislocation.[11] But no one questions the UN's central role in the successful conclusion of the peace talks. The UN was anxious to demonstrate its effectiveness in peacemaking and peacekeeping, given the concurrent fiascos in Bosnia and Somalia.

In July 1991, the UN launched ONUSAL (the United Nations Observers Mission to El Salvador) to oversee the implementation of the human rights agreement signed the previous year. While many social organisations in San Salvador hailed the arrival of ONUSAL as a 'popular victory', not everyone showed the same enthusiasm. Right-wing groups distributed flyers threatening the owners of exclusive restaurants with reprisals if they served members of this meddling mission. But ONUSAL soon became an established, if controversial, presence in El Salvador, setting the stage for an even wider post-war role. With unprecedented access to information and government officials, an annual budget of as much as $32 million, and almost complete freedom of movement for its team of over 1200 observers, ONUSAL had tremendous capacity to intervene in the implementation of the Peace Accord.

When the Land Transfer Programme stalled, ONUSAL set up a special commission to address bottlenecks in the assignment of titles. When voter registration problems threatened the viability of the 1994 elections, ONUSAL conducted endless high-level negotiations and directed its field staff to move people and documents around the country to improve registration tallies. When disgruntled ex-soldiers took over government buildings in January 1994, Chief of Mission Enrique ter Horst personally mediated negotiations between leaders of the ex-soldiers and the President. At least seven times during 1992 and 1993, Pérez de Cuellar's successor as Secretary-General, Boutros Ghali, sent in his personal representative, Marrack Goulding, to help untangle such problems.

ONUSAL involvement peaked at the time of the 1994 elections as the mission operated a special election division with hundreds of international observers. ONUSAL officially closed in April 1995, leaving behind a small technical mission, MINUSAL, which became the United Nations Verification Office. As the fifth anniversary of the Peace Accord approached, President Calderón Sol opposed the extension of the UN role, while the FMLN and other opposition sectors argued that the tenuous state of the transition continued to require the presence of a formal UN verification team. In December 1996, the UN officially closed its verification office in El Salvador, leaving behind a small staff reporting directly to the Secretary General's special envoy, Alvaro de Soto.

Was ONUSAL a success? The mission clearly helped the peace process over many rough spots, and maintained international attention on El Salvador during the immediate post-war period. Many Salvadorans have stories about ONUSAL observers driving their white Toyotas like maniacs through town, and no one could easily accept the idea of Mexican police being paid a small fortune to tell the Salvadorans how to solve their problems. At the same time, others speak of the UN policeman who brought their grandmother to the hospital or the young *chele* (white guy) who helped their sister get registered to vote. While they may not be able to say exactly how they helped, most Salvadorans feel that the presence of UN personnel made the post-war transition easier.

A second critical element of the UN mandate involved the consolidation of the new institutions created by the peace process, such as the National Civilian Police, the Office of the Human Rights Ombudsman, the Supreme Electoral Tribunal, and the National Council of the Judiciary. Predictably, this task proved even more challenging than achieving formal compliance with the main elements of the Chapultepec Accord. Even five years after the signing of the Accord, the extreme fragility of these institutions made an extension of the UN mandate a necessity.

Land: the unresolved problem

A group of campesinos has set up camp under pieces of plastic on the road leading to a large coffee plantation near Sonsonate. They recently occupied the plantation demanding land, but the police arrived and threatened them with arrest so they have set up this camp on the road.

One of the men, José Argueda, says bitterly: 'We thought the war, and then the peace, would make things better. But we've found that, in reality, there's nothing for us. The war brought us nothing and peace brought us nothing.'[12] Argueda and his fellow members of the ADC (Democratic Campesino Alliance) insist that the government has not fulfilled its Peace Accord pledges to complete the agrarian reform by distributing the land of farms over 245 hectares.

War in El Salvador had no single cause, but increasing landlessness and rural poverty during the 1960s and 1970s created the conditions for rural insurrection. As early as 1976, the military government of Gen. Arturo Molina attempted a timid experiment in land distribution, but opposition from the military and large landowners rendered the plan totally inoperative. Aware of the explosiveness of the land situation, in the late 1970s USAID began promoting a new plan to distribute land to poor campesinos. A complicated and contradictory set of laws provided for the redistribution of the land of all farms exceeding 500 hectares. With the support of the army, the land reform programme redistributed almost 20 per cent of the country's agricultural land, the majority of it to co-operatives made up primarily of families that had been working on these estates. Over 85,000 campesino families received land.

Using the intensification of the war as a pretext, the government failed to provide the co-operatives with the services necessary to make them viable productive units. Even though they controlled a significant percentage of the production of the country's most important exports, the co-operatives struggled throughout the war to resolve problems of credit, technical capacity, and organisation.

The war itself brought about further land transfers, as campesinos occupied abandoned estates. The Peace Accord set up a Land Transfer Programme (PTT) whereby such squatters, and ex-combatants from both sides, would be able to purchase land. Finally, the government committed itself to proceed with the long-overdue final phase of agrarian reform and redistribute the land of all estates over 245 hectares.

External donors provided the money for the PTT, but the government Land Bank was responsible for legal transfers, and its National Reconstruction Secretariat was to provide credit and technical assistance. The plan was for the PTT to distribute an average of 3.2 manzanas of land to 38,000 people.

Rhodri Jones/Oxfam

Distributing land through the PTT was a giant task, but creating the conditions for people to become viable farmers proved even more difficult. Even those lucky enough to receive PTT land often ended up with an impossible burden of land debt, housing debt, and short-term debt for productive inputs. In mid-1996, the government offered to forgive 70 per cent of the land debt of agrarian reform and PTT beneficiaries, provided that they could pay off the remaining 30 per cent within one year.

Farmers with relatively small amounts of debt, including most PTT beneficiaries, looked favourably on the offer, but few of the agrarian reform co-operatives could hope to come up with 30 per cent of a debt that had been accumulating interest since the early 1980s. They would have to sell off their most valuable land to make such a payment, and many saw the offer as a sophisticated attempt to get the best land back into the hands of wealthy Salvadorans. The debts of those unable to pay off the 30 per cent would be taken over by a private bank, empowered to foreclose in the event of continued failure to repay. This led one analyst to refer to the new measure as 'The Law of Guaranteed Foreclosure'.

Although land redistribution between the period 1980-92 distributed land to upwards of 100,000 families, USAID found that, at the end of the war, at least 370,000 adults in rural El Salvador still had little or no land.[13] In terms of rural poverty, the current situation is surprisingly similar to that immediately before the war.

Around the country, other ADC members occupied over 50 more properties. The government called for negotiations to solve the problem, but also passed laws toughening the penalties for illegal trespass on private property. The participants in the ADC action eventually packed up and headed back to the dismal conditions from which they had come, with little to show for their efforts. The government claimed to have resolved the 'threat'; but the problem of rural landlessness in El Salvador remains far from resolved.

Jenny Matthews/Oxfam

Jenny Matthews/Oxfam

Ending the war, constructing the peace

The euphoria surrounding the signing of the Peace Accord quickly became a shared enthusiasm for rebuilding the country. Demobilisation created much confusion and dislocation as people moved around the country seeking to re-enter civilian life. After so much sacrifice during the war, people wanted their economic situation to improve quickly after the signing of the peace. Talk of 'national reconstruction', however, puzzled the residents of the ex-conflictive zones. As one woman from the repatriated community of Nueva Esperanza remarked: 'I don't understand this talk about reconstruction. We never saw this place before the war...we're not reconstructing anything, but building something completely new.'

The international community offered financial support for the construction of peace in El Salvador. At a March 1992 World Bank Consultative Group meeting in Washington, donor governments led by the United States, the European Union, and Japan pledged over $800 million to support a National Reconstruction Plan (PRN) jointly presented by the Salvadoran government and the FMLN, to be implemented through the government's National Reconstruction Secretariat (SRN).

Many of the international NGOs that had been supporting emergency resettlement and subsistence economic projects during the war renewed those commitments for the construction of peace. They continued to channel the bulk of their funds directly

right Families displaced during the war, living in improvised shelters.

Mike Goldwater/Oxfam

26

Rhodri Jones / Oxfam

through local NGOs rather than through the SRN bureaucracy.

The SRN started work with a project to distribute a basic set of domestic goods to each demobilised combatant of the FMLN. Over the next few years, the SRN put in place a wide range of programmes, from agricultural training for those receiving land through the Land Transfer Programme to medical care for wounded war veterans. Critics, including a USAID evaluative team, pointed out many technical flaws and a lack of coordination in the SRN programmes.

The section of the Peace Accord referring to the PRN orients the reconstruction toward the 'integral development' of the ex-conflictive zones, a response to the immediate needs of the ex-combatants of both sides, and the repair of damaged infrastructure. With the government in command of implementation, national reconstruction took on quite a different hue. Beyond question, the government's economic programme and the political interests of the ruling ARENA party took precedence over any notion of integral development. The government sought firstly, to set up compensatory social programmes for ex-combatants that would avoid the re-emergence of armed

groups, as had occurred in neighbouring Nicaragua. Secondly, it embarked on a programme of public works to bring maximum political benefit to the ARENA party and minimise the benefits to opposition parties; and a programme of selective infrastructure repair to permit market forces to re-activate the economy of the war-affected regions. Above all, the PRN process had to fit into the overall economic programme of structural adjustment.[14]

A spokesperson of the World Bank described the PRN, in June 1995, as a 'remarkable success'. Not surprisingly, most of the intended beneficiaries of the PRN, and no small number of its donors, take a very different view.

Structural adjustment and 'remesanomics'

El Salvador's agroexport economy collapsed when war broke out. A combination of attacks on plantations, market changes, and an investment boycott by an oligarchy opposed to even the moderate reforms of the Christian Democrats, caused export income to plunge. The contribution of export agriculture to the economy shrunk from a high of 25 per cent in

1978 to 4 per cent in 1992. The United States aid programme, which accounted for as much as half of the government budget in the mid-1980s, could not prevent the country from slipping into a deep recession. While the political right vilified President Duarte for 'populist' policies, in fact real incomes of Salvadoran agricultural workers, for example, fell by 63 per cent between 1980 and 1991.

By the mid-1980s, however, a new source of foreign exchange had eclipsed both commodities and aid. El Salvador was exporting something of almost unlimited profitability: its people. The war had forced nearly one million Salvadorans to flee their country. While at least half of these emigrants ended up in the United States, significant numbers of Salvadorans also went to Canada, Australia, several European countries, Mexico, and neighbouring countries of Central America.

Wherever they were, the Salvadorans found work and began to send money to their relatives back home. The quantity of money (often in US dollars) sent back by these Salvadorans — *remesas* — became the only bright part of a gloomy economic picture. After reaching $120 million in 1984, remittances rose steadily until they passed a billion dollars in 1995, twice the income from exports.

When it took office in 1989, the Cristiani administration immediately embarked upon the ambitious structural adjustment programme that it had been planning for years. The plan included cuts in government subsidies of all sorts, privatisation of public entities including the banks, and tariff reductions and tax reforms, all designed to decrease state participation in the economy and to increase the role of the market. The programme sought to reorient the economy toward export activities, especially non-traditional exports like melons, shrimps, and textiles.

Few countries have had better economic conditions in which to implement structural adjustment. Even though the economy had been ravaged by the war, massive aid inflows from the US had kept it afloat by minimising balance-of-payments problems and foreign debts. While ARENA's strategy of 'outward-looking growth' encouraged any and all exports, the *maquila* sector accounted for much of the country's export growth, increasing from 18.3 per cent of exports in 1990, to 40 per cent in 1995. Nearly all Salvadoran *maquilas* involve textile production, much of it for well-known manufacturers like The Gap, Eddie Bauer, and Liz Claiborne.

Critics pointed out that volatile investments in *maquila* factories could leave El Salvador as quickly as they had come. Raw materials and machinery are imported, and Salvadoran labour used to assemble goods, so the plants represent relatively little value-added for the Salvadoran economy.[15] As the notoriously dismal labour conditions in the plants placed El Salvador back at the centre of international debate about labour rights, *maquilas* looked less and less like the path to long-term economic well-being.

Rhodri Jones /Oxfam

below Former President Alfredo Cristiani.

The government's commitment to structural adjustment found favour with the international financial institutions. In February 1991, the World Bank approved an initial structural adjustment loan for $75 million. In 1991-93 alone, the Bank and the Inter-American Development Bank (IADB) approved more than $800 million in loans to El Salvador. Each loan came with strings attached, deepening the country's commitment to structural adjustment whatever the social cost.

The implementation of structural adjustment had an almost immediate negative impact on the lives of poor Salvadorans. Increases in the prices of staple goods, such as rice, beans, cooking oil, and powdered milk, squeezed family budgets to the limits. Decreased tariffs threatened the tiny profit margins of a range of small and medium-sized businesses, and tax reform tended to redistribute income upward away from the poor. Even according to the government's own statistics, levels of extreme and relative poverty increased during the period 1989–91.

The private negotiations with the World Bank and other institutions occurred during the peace process, but the government remained adamant that its economic programme was not on the negotiating table, although the final agreement did contain a little section called 'Measures to Alleviate the Social Costs of Structural Adjustment Programmes'.

While the political scene shifted dramatically in the post-war period, the economic backdrop remained remarkably constant. As a nationwide programme of government action to respond to the extraordinary needs of constructing peace, the PRN threatened to sabotage structural

above Protestor, at the time of the arson attack widely believed to be the work of government agents, which destroyed the offices of *Diario Latino*, a left-wing newspaper.

adjustment by increasing fiscal deficits, creating new public agencies, or involving the government in propping up new economic agents, such as farmers in the ex-conflictive zones. However, the government shaped the PRN to avoid such sabotage. The vast majority of PRN funds would come from external sources, thus holding down deficits. The market would still decide who succeeded and who failed. There would be no subsidies or price supports for vegetables produced by ex-combatants, and co-operatives would not benefit from special marketing arrangements. (For example, the pre-war owners of the salt works would successfully prevent Usulutan co-operatives selling salt on the national market, for years.)

Like all apologists for the free market, the ARENA government could recognise the limits of the ideology when it affected ARENA constituents. The government quickly made the huge infrastructure investments that opened the way for the post-war construction boom in and around San Salvador; without roads, bridges, water and sewer services, the hills around San Salvador would be dotted with far fewer stunning new mansions. And when coffee prices plunged, threatening the income of an important ARENA constituency, the free-market government had no trouble agreeing to an export price subsidy of $15 per 200 lb. sack of the 'golden bean'.

The UN soon noticed the contradiction between its vision of the construction of peace and the World Bank's advocacy of strict structural adjustment. To describe the problem, Alvaro de Soto used the image of two surgical teams separated by a curtain as they operate on a patient (postwar El Salvador) without knowledge of each other's work.[16] De Soto advocated a tempering of structural adjustment in response to the special needs of the post-war period, while the Nordic group of donors to the PRN called for the World Bank to go a step further and pursue a 'peace conditionality' which would tie aid disbursements to compliance with the principal components of the Peace Accord.

The government showed some flexibility; it made necessary investments in some reconstruction programmes, such as credits for ex-combatants. Similarly, it eventually channelled funds to the PNC when it became clear that international donors were not prepared to bankroll the country's police force. In general, however, when the needs of constructing peace contradicted the dictates of structural adjustment, the latter prevailed.[17] In El Salvador, even the peace process has been structurally adjusted.

right The USA regarded El Salvador as part of its 'backyard'.

Rhodri Jones/Oxfam

The elections of the century

One of the principal agreements of the Peace Accord concerned the participation in elections of the entire political spectrum, including the FMLN. The first post-war elections in 1994 were seen as a measure of progress towards lasting peace.

Familiar forces threatened the elections when, in late 1993, illegal armed groups reminiscent of the death squads of the 1980s gunned down three prominent FMLN candidates, one of whom was killed in front of his daughter's nursery school as the three-year-old looked on. The UN had just announced that it would convene a special body to investigate these illegal armed groups, when the third of these killings took place. After this, however, visible violence subsided and the election campaign continued. In March, the country held simultaneous municipal, legislative, and presidential elections under the watchful eyes of thousands of electoral observers.

Armando Calderón Sol, candidate of the National Republican Alliance (ARENA) and former mayor of San Salvador, won the presidential race by a wide margin in a run-off against Rubén Zamora, candidate of an FMLN-led coalition. ARENA also maintained effective control of the Legislative Assembly and won 206 of 262 municipal elections. The electoral system favoured ARENA, which won 80 per cent of the local elections with 48 per cent of the votes. The left-wing coalition got a quarter of the votes, but won only 6 per cent of the mayoral elections. Observers and opposition parties alike cited evidence of widespread government abuses from the voter registration period through the post-election vote count.[18] ONUSAL, however, gave the elections qualified approval and the FMLN decided not to dispute the results.

Mark Chamberlain

Mark Chamberlain

above, top
FMLN/Convergencia Democratica/Movimiento Nacional (Left Wing Coalition) End of Campaign Rally, San Salvador, 11 March 1994.

above Voting station, Mejicaños, San Salvador, 20 March, 1994.

Mark Chamberlain

Mark Chamberlain

above, top FMLN Rally in front of San Salvador Cathedral, San Salvador, 11 March 1994.

above FMLN Worker campaigning in Zacamil, San Salvador.

The election results, especially at the local level, surprised political commentators. How could a party of the extreme right such as ARENA have defeated a popular movement like the FMLN? The Frente's defeat was attributed to a combination of its inexperience and ARENA's far greater financial resources; but other factors also contributed.

ARENA was formed in 1981, shortly after the creation of the FMLN, by a small number of right-wing zealots, followers of Roberto D'Aubuisson. Numerous investigations, including that of the post-war Truth Commission, connect D'Aubuisson and his ARENA cohorts with death-squad killings in that early period.[19]

ARENA became an extremely effective political organisation. It could count on a solid base of nearly a quarter of the electorate that wholeheartedly supported its right-wing policies. D'Aubuisson did well in the 1982 elections, and would have been elected president by the Constitutional Assembly but for the direct intervention of the US Ambassador. His supporters came from all social groups, demonstrating the intense polarisation of Salvadoran society. Party adherents idolised D'Aubuisson, and supported the death squads as a necessary antidote to 'communist subversion'. While the FMLN could legitimately claim to be a mass social movement, the extreme right also had a mass following.

By the time of the 1994 elections, ARENA had managed to attract a large number of more moderate supporters, while keeping much of their conservative base. These new supporters, also from varied socioeconomic backgrounds, saw benefits for themselves in the ARENA economic programme and optimistic vision for the future. Some supporters feared that an FMLN election victory would plunge the country back into conflict and instability. ARENA exploited this fear in their pre-election TV blitz.

ARENA also made clever use of public resources; advertisements for government reconstruction programmes became, in effect, ARENA propaganda. More importantly, ARENA directed the money spent by the SRN so as to maximise its political gains and minimise the FMLN's efforts to build political capital through the reconstruction process.

The FMLN entered the elections at a decided disadvantage. The Frente's new party organisation was weak and ineffectual. Internal bickering among its constituent groups made almost every decision a struggle and cost the Frente dearly in the public relations battle. Finally, in one municipality after another, the FMLN violated the cardinal rule of local politics by failing to choose candidates who were well-known and trusted. ARENA also used every conceivable legitimate and illegitimate way of making it as difficult as possible for the Frente to register its supporters and get them to the polls, especially in the rural areas. Given the many procedural irregularities, the exclusion of so many potential voters from voting, and the decision of half of all eligible voters to stay at home, the Central American University dubbed the elections 'the fiasco of the century'.

In retrospect, however, even the FMLN admits that ARENA's 'soft fraud' only influenced the outcome of perhaps twenty-five local elections, and one legislative contest.

In the wake of the elections, the Salvadoran political parties underwent major changes as the alliances of the war years were reviewed. Both the Christian Democratic Party and the FMLN split in two, giving the impression of a weak and divided opposition. ARENA also suffered considerable internal tensions, and, while it did not split, several key party members defected to other parties just before the 1997 elections. The FMLN and other opposition parties took the lessons of 1994 to heart in preparing for the 1997 elections.

Remaking local government

The Spanish colonial government established municipalities in its colonies as a way of extending its administrative control. In El Salvador, 262 municipalities of varying shapes and sizes were created, only the largest of which had significant resources. Local politics has always mirrored the corruption and authoritarianism of the national system: the wise mayor maintained close relations with wealthy families and the commander of the local garrison. The Salvadoran electoral system was one of 'winner-take-all' in which the mayor's party holds all the posts in the municipal council.

far left Page from *Guide to the Elections*, published by Hombres de Maiz, 1994.

left Training international election observers at the Centre for International Solidarity

Mark Chamberlain

Mark Chamberlain

33

right
Party representatives
at voting table on
election day, Suchitoto,
20 March 1994.

During the war the national government and USAID identified the mayors as crucial for their counter-insurgency campaign. The US-sponsored MIA (Municipalities in Action) programme poured millions of dollars into public works projects carried out through the mayors. The FMLN responded with coercive pressure against mayors thought to be using project funds to build support for the government war-effort. The Frente assassinated several of them and forced dozens of others to govern from outside their municipalities. In some conflictive regions, the municipal structure ceased to function.

Despite the intense polarisation at the local level, the government and USAID decided to distribute post-war reconstruction funds through municipalities. After the signing of the Peace Accord, one of the first tasks of ONUSAL became the delicate negotiations around the return of mayors to municipalities from which they had been 'exiled'.

During the 1994 elections, FMLN candidates proposed a 'new municipalism' that would break with the exclusionary past and create a truly participatory local politics; but, to the surprise of even ARENA, the FMLN won only 15 municipalities, even failing to win several municipalities in Chalatenango and Morazán that they had effectively controlled during the war.

Miriam Chicas of Perquín, Morazán was the only woman among the fifteen victorious mayoral candidates of the FMLN. Being elected mayor was the 'biggest surprise' for Miriam. She began with great enthusiasm, but halfway through her first term her face shows signs of tension and fatigue.

Asked about her general impression of her tenure as mayor, she says 'We're tired, nothing comes easy, but we're a long way from giving up.' José Rufino Díaz, mayor of Arambala, and José Ismael Romero Hernández, mayor of Jocoatique, nod their heads in agreement.

'The government has forgotten about areas like northern Morazán, and it doesn't matter if you are an ARENA mayor or from the opposition. All we are doing is finishing projects started by the previous mayor,' explains Miriam. 'The SRN says that USAID is holding up the money destined to support new projects here, but I went on a trip to Washington and they told me the opposite.' Both USAID and the SRN insist that municipalities in the ex-conflictive zones have received a fair proportion of project funds. In fact, according to SRN records, between April 1994 and June 1995 the eight municipalities in northern Morazán received just three new projects.

The mayors say that they have learned how to work together, and have been able to develop effective mechanisms for participation. But without the funds to carry out projects, participation can just lead to frustration. For the mayor of Arambala: 'People come to meetings and propose projects, but when the projects don't get supported, they start to blame us for things not getting done.'

Since USAID has now closed down its MIA programme, the question of where funding will come from for municipal development requires a long-term answer. Over one-third of El Salvador's 262 municipalities have populations of less than two thousand people and simply may not be economically viable. One option for funding is for local government to raise money through taxes. 'That's a good idea, but who are we going to tax here?' asks Miriam. 'The rich all left Perquín, and only we poor people are left.' The mayors hope central government will devote part of its increased tax income to a revenue-sharing plan, but wonder about the decision to direct the money through the SRN. 'Those funds are the only way out for us,' says José Hernández, 'but what will be left after she [SRN Director Norma de Dowe] gets done paying all her big salaries and buying her cars?' (In late 1996, Norma de Dowe resigned, amid allegations of serious misuse of funds.)

The election of mayors like Miriam Chicas – totally unthinkable even five years ago – shows that something has changed in local politics. But the investment in the creation of democratic institutions at the national level has not been reflected in the municipalities. After the elections, all parties agreed to replace the 'winner-take-all' formula with a type of proportional representation on the municipal councils. Within a year, however, ARENA and its allies backed away from the proposal saying that the country's democracy was too young for such a change. Privately, ARENA leaders admitted that their mayors did not want proportional representation.

In spite of the difficulties, activists push forward with their efforts to create more democratic structures at the local level. In the wake of the positive results of municipal elections held in 1997, they have more reason than ever to believe their efforts will bear fruit.

Challenges for the millenium

The second elections of the post-war period occurred in March 1997, when the country went to the polls to elect the 84 members of the National Assembly and all 262 mayors. To the surprise of many observers, the FMLN did much better than it had in 1994 and support for the ARENA party declined precipitously. With its campaign criticising national economic policy and highlighting corruption in the ruling party, the FMLN won 27 legislative seats (only one seat less than ARENA). Either on its own or in coalition with other opposition parties, it gained control of 53 municipalities. After its triumphs in San Salvador and most of the other more populous municipalities, the FMLN will control the local governments of more Salvadorans than any other party. Stunned by the reversals at the local level, President Calderon Sol announced after the elections that ARENA was ready to reconsider the 'winner-take-all' formula in municipal elections.

The results pointed to increasing discontent with ARENA's economic approach and highlighted divisions within the ruling party. Several important party leaders, including Alfredo Cristiani's Vice-President, either formed new parties or shifted to existing right-wing alternatives.

Even though the FMLN did not make its gains based on a programme of substantive social change, the elections served as a hopeful sign for many Salvadorans seeking such change. In the wake of the victory celebration in Soyapango, one jubilant FMLN supporter commented 'Even ARENA knows that if the Frente can make good use of the local power it has won today, it will be easy to win the presidency in 1999.'

The results, therefore, challenge the country's traditional ruling groups to maintain support for a system in which they may lose political control. At the same time, the gains of 1997 challenge the FMLN and its allies to prove that, within that system, they can achieve changes that benefit El Salvador's poor majority.

Something new in post-war El Salvador

Katalina Aneca

Jenny Matthews / Oxfam

The first time she arrived at Villa Victoria's ramshackle City Hall for a meeting with the town's ARENA mayor, Vilma Sanchez's legs trembled uncontrollably. The local coordinator of Women for Life and Dignity (the DIGNAS) had no idea how the mayor would react to a group of women representing rural communities associated with the FMLN during the war.

Vilma and her *compañeras* presented a 'municipal platform' developed by women in meetings throughout the municipality. Highlighting the poverty faced by the women and their families, they demanded local government projects to bring electricity and safe drinking water to each community, and to provide health and educational facilities. The DIGNAS met the mayors of six municipalities in different areas, all but one located in the ex-conflictive areas served by El Salvador's National Reconstruction Plan (PRN). The initiative represents a radical departure in a country with no tradition of participation by the poor in local politics, let alone a group of poor women. Predictably, not all of the mayors were welcoming.

In Villa Victoria, however, the mayor has been surprisingly open to discussions of the proposals. Although no projects have yet resulted from the initiative, according to Vilma: 'It is important that our work has been recognised, and that the mayor now involves us in discussions with other local authorities. And we've gotten over our fears,' she adds with a smile.

Who's poor in El Salvador?

As in most developing countries, women in El Salvador bear a disproportionate share of the burden of poverty. The country's woefully inadequate health system, for example, is unable to respond to the specific health needs of women. Only 609 maternal hospital beds are available for the 150,000 births that take place each year. In 1992, 70 per cent of all mothers had no prenatal care of any sort and El Salvador had one of the highest rates of maternal mortality in Latin America. The Ministry of Health reports that in 1991, 70 per cent of all its out-patient consultations for anaemia were with women.

For a whole variety of cultural and economic reasons, women have less access to formal employment than men. The culture of *machismo* continues to project a powerful ideal of the Salvadoran woman, living in the private sphere of the home under the protection of her husband. *Machismo* is the rationale behind job discrimination, domestic violence, and women's limited participation in social organisations. The experience of the civil war undermined these cultural patterns in many ways, but affirmed them in others.

Employers are more than happy to conform with the cultural norms of *machismo*. Discrimination excludes women from many jobs, and results in women being paid less than men. The *maquila* textile assembly plants have become one of the few sources of employment for women. The factories have gained international notoriety for low wages, inhumane working conditions, and the mistreatment of women workers by their male supervisors. But with few or no other options, women continue to take these jobs; recently, however, they have begun to unionise to improve pay and working conditions.

Most women can not find work, even in the *maquilas*. Hundreds of thousands of them work in the 'informal sector' as street vendors of everything under the sun, as domestics in the homes of wealthy and middle-class Salvadorans, and by doing anything else that will enable them to feed their children. This sector of the economy is growing, but long hours of hard labour do not guarantee even a survival income.

Official poverty statistics, which measure household income against the cost of basic consumer goods, show that in 1993, just under 60 per cent of Salvadoran families did not have sufficient income to buy basic necessities. But

Jenny Matthews /Oxfam

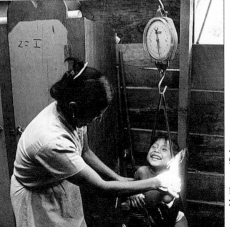

Jenny Matthews /Oxfam

Jenny Matthews /Oxfam

above Young girl helping with the housework.

and toddlers, then begin working themselves, rather than going to school. Either home becomes a part of the workplace, or women take their family life with them to the streets, in a full-time struggle for survival.

The rise of gender politics

During the war, Salvadoran women, both in women's organisations and alongside men in mixed ones, carried out many crucial tasks. They did not, however, succeed in focusing attention on the particular needs and capacities of women. Referring to that time, Isabel Guevara of the MSM (Salvadoran Women's Movement) says: 'We had not yet defined ourselves as a movement...we were not clear about our role.' Women were not encouraged to raise issues of sexual equality. Vilma Sanchez insists: 'They'd tell you, no! First we must sort out the oppression of the rich over the poor...the women's problems will come later on.'

When the war ended, many women were prepared to form a new kind of women's movement, one that would place the needs and capacities of women at the centre of its agenda. Morena Herrera of Las Dignas talks about the broadening of her vision when she first saw the potential of this sort of a movement: 'I went [to an international meeting in Argentina] and I have to say that I just fell in love with feminism. It gave me a way to move my individual rebellion into collective rebellion... just like the Frente had done for me almost fifteen years before.'

Women's organisations grew quickly and they formed networks like the *Concertación de Mujeres* (Women's Coalition). Contacts with women from other countries also helped to build the confidence of Salvadoran feminists.

The word '*género*' was increasingly used as women identified power relations between men and women as an important source of El Salvador's social problems. Part of the solution to the problem of poverty was seen to be a change in patterns of resource distribution within families. Women also asserted that state programmes designed to meet the needs of rural women would have more impact in overcoming poverty. As the

statistics shed little light on the 'feminisation of poverty'. Because of unequal power relations between women and men, in many families available resources are not shared equally among family members. Furthermore, government statistics do not distinguish between female-headed households — the majority in many poor communities in El Salvador — and those with a male breadwinner, and thus underestimate poverty among women and children.

The problem of poverty is neither an abstract nor statistical concept for Salvadoran women. They must confront its all-too-real face every day as they seek to provide for their families. The length of their working day increases, and a day of rest at home with the family becomes an elusive luxury. Children accompany their mothers at work as infants movement incorporated this gender perspective, it focused less on the 'plight of women' and more on the capacity of organised women to change their situation.

Salvadoran women do not romanticise their movement. They acknowledge a range of problems linked to the sectarian and authoritarian wartime conditions. 'I'm not going to lie to you,' says one leading woman activist, 'we have women from the FPL and the RN in here, two of the groups that clashed the most during the war. We still have serious conflicts, that sometimes make me wonder if I can continue with this. But the fact that we are all here means that we want to try to put that behind us.'

Prior to the 1994 elections, *Mujeres '94* (Women '94) held together dozens of women's groups long enough to draft 'The Salvadoran Women's Platform': the only comprehensive political programme produced by any social sector during the campaign. By compelling the political parties to respond to it, 'Women '94' significantly raised the profile of the women's movement.

In these early years, women's organis-ations struggled for the political and financial autonomy to plan and carry out their own programmes. Silvia Matus of MAM (Melida Anaya Montes Women's Movement) explains: '[International NGOs] should leave it up to women's groups, with all their limitations and potential, to assume responsibility for the design, administration and execution of programmes.'[20] Where women have gained control of resources, they have organised a dizzying array of activities that have in common a desire to empower women to overcome everyday problems, including those associated with poverty. They offered young women recreational opportunities, like softball; organised health clinics for women and children; designed programmes to offer counselling and other support to battered women; and set in motion local credit schemes to allow women to become viable producers.

None of the leaders of even the most successful women's projects harbour the illusion that these, alone, can counter the powerful global forces affecting the poor everywhere. But in challenging the historic isolation and powerlessness of poor women in El Salvador, such projects represent new hope for the future.

left Making tortillas is a time-consuming task which has to be done every day.

Teresa's story

Almost all working Salvadorans get some days off to celebrate 6 August, the feast of Jesus Christ, Saviour of the World, the patron saint that gives the country its name. By mid-day on 5 August, very few people are working.

On Saturday, 5 August, I head south from San Salvador, along the coastal highway. I pass the giant, new *El Pedregal* 'free zone' located on what used to be open pasture land. I'm amazed at how much the free zone has expanded since the last time I saw it in January.

The road stretches out straight, hot and empty on this vacation day for everyone, even the bus drivers. Near Zacatecoluca, a woman jumps into the road to flag me down for a lift. Knowing that there are no buses, I stop.

Teresa, her sister Daysi, and four children pile into the back seat of the jeep. Teresa is talkative, and tells me she is on her way to Jiquilísco, a city in Usulután very near where I am going.

She works at a factory in the free-zone. A *gringo* named Peter owns it, and they make plastic gloves for hospitals in the United States.

What are you doing on the road today, when there are no buses?

He just let us out at noon. We work a half-day on Saturday, and then I had to go to Zacate to pick up Daysi and the kids.

Even today, on the holiday?

We were afraid that they'd make us work longer today.

Teresa earns 1050 colones per month (about $120, the minimum wage for factory work in El Salvador). But after deductions, she only takes home 483 colones every 15 days. After three months at the factory, she still does not know exactly what is being deducted, and she doesn't plan to ask.

It's not good to make trouble. The gringo is a nice guy, but some of the Salvadorans he has working there are really mean.

What do they do that's mean?

They shout at the girls, and hit them sometimes. And you know that if you don't do what they want, you won't be working there...and they make you stand up...all day long, standing up with the gloves. That's the worst part.

Teresa works nine hours each weekday, and five hours on Saturday: fifty hours a week. That makes her salary about 50 cents an hour.

What's the best thing about the job?

The best thing...I'm working, so I have some money to buy some clothes for these kids. And they have something to eat, even if it's just tortillas and beans. Lots of people can't do that.

Do you work at the factory, too, Daysi?

No...I work in Zacate.

Daysi is not nearly as talkative as her sister.

What do you do?

.....She's a muchacha in the house of a man who works for the government. [Teresa answering for Daysi]

That's a long way to come to work in somebody else's house.

Yes, it's pretty far, but I can go home with the kids on Saturday.

They pay her 250 colones [$28.75 a month] and she can have the kids there...all the kids, mine, too...and the woman lets me sleep there, too, if I buy the food.

Adds Teresa.

Daysi finally gets a word in edgewise:

And Teresa says that I might be able to get a job at the factory. They hire more girls sometimes and she's going to tell me when.

By now we are approaching the turn-off to Jiquilísco. Before Teresa gets out, she asks me how much it will be for her, Daysi, and the kids. She smiles gratefully when I simply thank her for her company.

below Women workers in a clothing factory. Women work long hours for low pay in the free-zone factories.

Linda Miller/Oxfam

An overdue look at the environment

During El Salvador's civil war, relatively little public debate on the country's ecological condition took place. A few groups were formed, such as CESTA, the Salvadoran Centre for Appropriate Technology, to address conservation and other environmental issues, but they had little impact. After the signing of the Peace Accord, attention turned at last to the ecological crisis that had been building since long before the war, in particular the complex relationship between water shortage, deforestation, and erosion.

A long line of women and children waiting to draw drinking water from a public tap had become a common sight during the war. The government had always claimed the shortages resulted from guerrilla sabotage of the electrical system. In early 1995, near the end of the dry season, stories circulated throughout El Salvador about angry confrontations among individuals and communities asserting conflicting claims to the decreasing amount of water bubbling from declining numbers of natural springs. Almost every day another neighbourhood in the capital claimed that it had gone four, five, or more days without water. All of the major newspapers carried regular stories on the water problem and speculated about the roots of the problem, now it could no longer be blamed on FMLN sabotage.

Around the same time, campesinos from the hamlets of Los Morales and Platanares near Nombre de Jesús, Chalatenango, almost came to machete blows to settle a water dispute. Hearing of the near-tragedy, Father Bruno Ambrosini, parish priest of Nombre de Jesús, observed sadly: 'They fought this war over land: the next one is going to be over water.' He echoed the increasingly common observation that, unless the water system is 'fixed', control over a dwindling water supply is likely to become a source of serious social conflict.

Rhodri Jones/Oxfam

The Lempa River and its tributaries is one of Central America's largest river systems, and contains 60 per cent of the country's total water supply, and drains well over half of the land area. By the beginning of the twentieth century, the hills and valleys on either side of the Lempa had been almost cleared of their original forest cover, for cultivation and human settlement.

above The shortage of water is becoming an increasing problem in El Salvador.

Deforestation has continued as poor campesinos have cleared even the steepest hillsides to plant corn, and have cut more trees in the search of their primary fuel source, wood. The entire area is now almost totally devoid of forest cover.

The absence of trees makes the land less able to absorb the abundant rains of the six-month 'winter', thereby limiting the recharging of underground water sources. Springs that used to give water all year around now disappear midway through the dry season. Deforestation also increases the danger that wind, and water run-off, will carry away precious topsoil. Today, there are few hillsides in the Upper Lempa unaffected by erosion. SEMA (the government's environmental secretariat) estimates that the country loses the equivalent of 4,550 hectares of topsoil each year. For campesinos, erosion and deforestation significantly decrease agricultural output, make wood more expensive in time and effort (if not money), and decrease the dry-season availability of water for family needs and animal maintenance. Nationally, the ground water level is dropping at the rate of one metre a year. The ecological problems increase the pressure on livelihoods already marginal.

For nearly a generation, campesinos in El Salvador have used herbicides, pesticides and chemical fertilisers to boost corn yields on depleted and eroded soils. While solving some of the campesino's problems in the short run, dependence on agricultural chemicals has created many others, damaging the rural ecosystem and reducing bio-diversity. Faced with dramatic increases in the cost of inputs, many Salvadoran campesinos no longer see increased chemical use as a sustainable strategy.

The water problems of the Lempa basin are also starting to cramp urban lifestyles. El Salvador gets 60 per cent of its electricity from two large hydroelectric dams on the Lempa, and the nation's energy security plan calls for five smaller dams to be constructed in the next two decades. The topsoil washed into the river through erosion settles to the bottom of the artificial lakes serving the dams, reducing their capacity. This, in turn, reduces the capacity of the dam to generate electricity, while the sediment increases the maintenance costs. When residents in the capital received constantly increasing electric bills during the mid-1990s, they were, in part, paying the cost of erosion in the Lempa Basin.

In the last decade, exponential increases in demand for water — along with steady drops

Jenny Matthews/Oxfam

in the water table around the capital —have caused San Salvador to look beyond its own considerable underground supplies. Massive projects have been designed to pump water to San Salvador from the artificial lakes of the Lempa. The same silt that fills the lakes and troubles power generating equipment also fouls the state-of-the-art pumping equipment, thus raising serious questions about the viability of such schemes.

The central hydrological role of the Lempa River has, therefore, linked the living standards of urban users of electrical and water services to the agricultural practices of campesinos scraping a living from the hillsides.

Non-governmental organisations (NGOs) concerned with these issues, such as PRISMA (the Salvadoran Environmental Research Project) and FUNDALEMPA (the Lempa River Foundation) see no solution to national short-falls of water and electrical supply without an enormous investment in integrated development programmes for the peasant farmers of the Lempa Basin. SEMA and FUSADES (the Salvadoran Foundation for Economic and Social Development), a private sector foundation closely tied to the ARENA party, are slowly coming to similar conclusions, although much of the private sector still believes that the market will drive small farmers away from the Lempa before the situation becomes truly critical.

The farmers of the Lempa Basin are well aware that their agricultural practices are undermining their own livelihoods, but confronted with a daily struggle for survival they see no alternative. One experienced international volunteer says: 'They see the deforestation and the erosion and notice that there is less water around every year, but if they don't plant the hillsides their families starve. Given the choice between hunger today and thirst in the future, people keep planting steeper hills.'

The development of effective soil conservation techniques and alternatives to hillside agriculture will take time and considerable financial resources. Large-scale reforestation of areas now under cultivation is technically possible but not socially feasible unless people are given options other than forced displacement programmes.

Santiago's land: hope along the Lempa

Santiago's land slopes steeply down to the Lempa River. He inherited his land from his father and grandfather before him. As a boy he learned about farming from his father who taught him the complex subtleties of planting and harvesting corn using techniques and technologies that had been passed from one generation to the next for over a thousand years.

The situation in Santiago's village, Hacienda Vieja, deteriorated following the assassination of Monseñor Romero in 1980. The National Guard began patrolling the area, capturing anyone suspected of guerrilla sympathies or merely pointed out by informers. One of Santiago's closest friends was taken away by the Guard, and found two days later floating in the Lempa tied to a mule, both man and mule with bullet holes in their heads.

One day, the local National Guard commander appeared in the town and gave the people twenty-four hours to leave; anyone who stayed behind would be shot. Santiago, 23 years old, had recently married Reina, 17. When the order came to leave, Reina was five months pregnant with their first child. It was November, the time of year to collect the corn

harvest now well dried and ready for storage. Almost all of Santiago's available cash had been invested in the corn field, or *milpa*.

Leaving meant financial ruin, but the residents of Hacienda Vieja took the National Guard's threat seriously. No one stayed in town past the deadline. They all hurriedly packed what they could carry on their shoulders, and fled to La Virtud, Honduras, a three-hour walk over the mountains. For over a year Santiago and Reina lived with a Honduran family.

Fearing that the Salvadorans along the border were aiding the guerrillas, the Honduran government and UNHCR decided to move the refugees to Mesa Grande, a large refugee camp further from the border. They were loaded into trucks, once again only able to take what they could carry, and taken to Mesa Grande, joining 11,500 other refugees from El Salvador's mountainous north.

In 1984, Santiago's and Reina's longing for home overcame their fears. With no support from the UNHCR or any other institution, they loaded up their few belongings and, with three other families, quietly returned to their village.

They were well aware of the risks they ran.

below Santiago in his milpa.

Their region had become one of the most conflictive areas of the country, occupied by the army and the FMLN, but controlled by neither. The army occupied a permanent position five miles from their village. Every time Santiago or Reina went to the market in Ilobasco, they were ordered off the bus and forced to queue up to show their identification. The army used such identity checks as a form of recruitment, forcibly taking away any male between the age of 15 and 25 who had not served his obligatory term in the army.

Their village, Hacienda Vieja, was barely recognisable. The church had been bombed, the water and electrical systems were in ruins, and thick weeds covered the only paved street. If the war had not destroyed a house, then neglect had left it barely habitable. All had been ransacked, robbed of anything of value, including the corn stored in small silos.

Within two or three years, all 45 of the original families had returned to Hacienda Vieja to plant their *milpas*, raise their children, and live the life that was familiar to them. Most of this informal repatriation took place well before the celebrated, UN-sponsored returns from the Honduran camps.

Today, at first glance, Santiago and Reina live very much as they did before the war. The rhythms of campesino culture, governed by the yearly cycle of planting and harvesting corn, are, however, under threat. Prominent among these threats are state economic policies that undercut small-scale, subsistence producers. The herbicides and pesticides that Santiago buys are more expensive every year. And because of the elimination of price supports and trade barriers, the price at which Santiago sells his small amount of surplus corn declines each year.

Campesinos are left with no alternative but to cultivate more and more acreage. Aware of the catastrophic ecological consequences of this search for survival, Santiago knows he is contributing to the premature death of a culture that has existed for over a thousand years. The region is almost entirely deforested, and precious topsoil washes away with every pounding rain storm. Within ten years it is probable that Santiago's land will not be able to sustain his children. He sees his *milpa* produce less each year, he sees the streams that never used to dry up during the dry season now parched by the end of the summer, so that cattle die of thirst, and he watches his wife and children carry water every day from the village's diminished water tank.

'I want my children to be able to live as we have,' Santiago says looking out over his *milpa* along the Lempa. 'Twenty years ago we all began using chemical fertilisers and we all saw a big difference in the amount of corn our milpas could produce. At that time the streams here were full of several kinds of fish and crabs. Now they are completely empty of life, we know that we have a serious problem with the land and the water, and we know that time is running out.'

Last year, Santiago began experimenting with making his own organic fertiliser. He collected animal droppings and mixed them with other organic materials. He produced enough organic fertiliser to conduct an experiment: fertilising part of his plot with the organic mix to see how it compared with the chemical fertiliser. 'I fertilised the section which has always produced the poorest corn, with the organic mix. [This year] the corn cobs are big and numerous, and I am convinced that organic fertiliser works as well if not better than chemical fertiliser.'

By making his own fertiliser, Santiago was able to save a little money; he may possibly break even this year. If successful in the long term, Santiago will have broken an addiction to chemical fertilisers that has left both people and land impoverished. 'Next year I hope to fertilise an even bigger portion of my *milpa*,' he says. Having seen his harvest, even the most sceptical local farmers are asking Santiago about his methods.

Santiago is contributing in his small way to building a sustainable agriculture that will allow the land to recuperate from years of chemical herbicides and fertilisers. 'Without land and water we cannot grow our food. Without the ability to grow our *milpas*, our way of life is over, and we will have to go elsewhere to find work.' Santiago and his family have already had to leave Hacienda Vieja once, and they don't intend to do so again.

All eyes on El Espino

Before the ink even dried on the Chapultepec Accord, many investors were preparing to reap the bonanza arising from the pent-up demand for commercial and residential development around San Salvador. The ecological impact of such speculation was of little concern. The case of Finca El Espino, a coffee plantation on the outskirts of San Salvador, revealed the contradiction between unbridled development and conservation, and thrust ecological issues into the national policy debate.[21]

Even during the war, the urban sprawl of San Salvador threatened the 808 hectares of coffee planted at Finca El Espino, virtually the last undeveloped strip between the capital and the neighbouring city of Santa Tecla. The *finca* runs up the side of the San Salvador volcano, where it meets other large coffee plantations. Occupying a prime site along the Pan-American highway, it also borders San Benito, one of the capital's most exclusive neighbourhoods.

The Dueñas family, one of El Salvador's richest, owned and operated El Espino as a highly-profitable coffee enterprise for nearly a century. In 1980 the land was handed over to a co-operative comprised mostly of workers on the property, under agrarian reform legislation. The co-operative faced many financial and administrative difficulties, but managed to harvest coffee every year during the war. However, they never acquired clear title to the land. El Espino served as a major thoroughfare for guerrillas moving between bases on the San Salvador volcano and targets in San Salvador and Santa Tecla.

The very moment the bullets stopped flying, however, the value of this land exploded. The Dueñas family quickly convinced their friends in government that they still had a legal claim to the land. In 1991, the government pulled off a manoeuvre that was outrageous, even by Salvadoran standards. They transferred the land back to the Dueñas family, and then agreed to buy back part of it for several times more than the family had received for it in 1980. The family planned to sell some of the remainder at an enormous profit to another family of the oligarchy, the Poma family, for commercial development.

The deal immediately became a focus of national attention. The co-operative alleged that the sale represented a gift to the old oligarchy and an effort to roll back agrarian reform; while environmental groups claimed that covering El Espino with concrete would be an ecological disaster. The forest cover of El Espino was critical to the land's ability to absorb the winter rains, and the recharging of the underground aquifer which was the primary water source for the metropolis.

A coalition of social and political groupings formed the Committee for the Defense of El Espino, and the arguments raged for more than three years. During debates in the Legislative Assembly, virtually every political figure in the country attempted to use the situation to their advantage. Meanwhile, coalition members were accusing each other of opportunism. While much of the public discussion focused on the ecological aspects, powerful economic and political forces were at work behind the scenes. By 1995, a compromise was reached whereby the Dueñas family would be allowed to sell part of the land for development, the co-operative would get clear title to another section, and the rest would become a municipally-owned park.

A year later all sides were back in court accusing each other of failure to abide by the agreement. Co-operative leaders, stung by accusations that they had 'sold themselves, like Judas, for a few gold coins' to rich families, stiffened their resolve to hold the government and the Dueñas family to their commitments. While a court order halted development temporarily, few believed that it could be stalled for long.

The tangled mesh of the El Espino case says much about the balance of power in post-war El Salvador. The fact the case became the subject of public controversy marks a change from the pre-war days when families like Dueñas and Poma dictated national policy. Regardless of its outcome, the affair created an unprecedented level of debate on ecological issues, increasing public awareness of the dangers of deforestation, and the delicate balance that conserves the country's water supply.

The high cost of health and education

Perspiration covers Napo's face and terror fills his eyes as he rushes toward the Roman Catholic church in Tierra Blanca, Usulután. In his arms, he carries his one-year-old daughter, Angelita. The baby's eyes are open, but rolling back into her head. Her skin is absolutely pale and strangely cool and dry given the intense, coastal heat. After taking one look at Napo, Sister Elena hurries back into her residence behind the church. 'Wait here, I'll be right back,' she says, in Spanish, over her shoulder. Moments later, she returns with a wad of local currency amounting to $60, a great sum of money for Napo. She asks a visiting friend, 'Will you take Napo and the baby into the private clinic in Usulután? He can tell you where it is. Don't let them keep you waiting. Just tell the nurse that the baby is dehydrated. The money should be enough to get her treated.'

The breathless father can say only, '*Gracias, hermana, muchas gracias*' as he and Angelita pile into an ancient Toyota jeep. Sister Elena explains to me that only the week before, Napo and his wife had buried Angelita's twin sister. Because the local health post had no medicine, the baby's mother had taken her to the regional hospital 25 miles away. After hours of waiting, she was told that the baby would be fine with a few pills. The child died on the way back to Tierra Blanca. 'We could never give money to all of the people in Napo's situation, but I felt I needed to do something in this case...I wasn't surprised to see him here with the baby.'

Two hours later, the jeep rattles back into town with a relieved father carrying Angelita, who no longer looks on the point of death. She is still very ill, but oral rehydration has begun to replace her bodily fluids, and with simple antibiotics she will recover from her intestinal infection. She was treated at the clinic only because her father had the money provided by Elena. In the absence of viable local health care

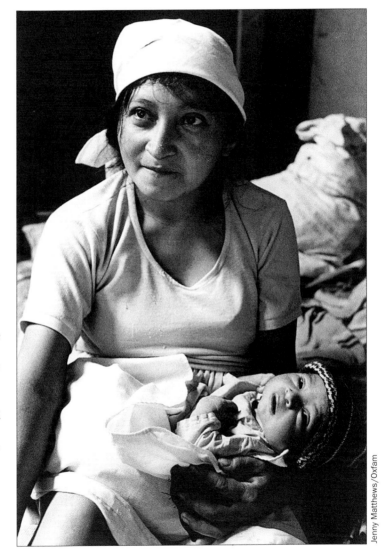

services, Elena will make regular visits to Napo's house to try to determine the cause of the illnesses.

At a retreat centre fifty miles west of Tierra Blanca in the department of La Libertad, the large meeting hall vibrates with a hundred excited voices. The young people gathered

above Childhood in El Salvador is a dangerous time: only 20 per cent of people in rural areas have access to health services, and many children die from diseases which would be easily treatable.

Jenny Matthews/Oxfam

here are the 'popular' teachers from small local communities. Many of them are under the age of 20 and few have attained even a fifth grade education. They work with nongovernmental organisations (NGOs), and are the primary hope for the education of the thousands of children living in those areas of the country where the public education system ceased to function during the war.

The teachers have gathered here with NGO coordinators with three goals in mind: to share teaching techniques and experiences; to discuss how they should relate to the Ministry of Education in reestablishing public education in their communities; to consider how they can gain the certificates necessary for recognition as professional teachers. Most of all, they are enjoying the chance to get to know each other after years of isolation. Two days later, they will be back in their communities teaching children, with few materials and little pay.

The health emergency in Tierra Blanca and the teachers' meeting in La Libertad illustrate the dismal state of basic service provision in post-war El Salvador, and the ways in which local organisations are responding. Poor health and education services, especially in rural areas, contributed to the intolerable social conditions that gave rise to the civil war.

During the war, public services disappeared altogether from those areas of the country not under government control, and the diversion of resources to the war effort caused further decay of services elsewhere. When the Cristiani administration began to implement its structural adjustment programme in 1989, the government's already meagre expenditures for health and education were further reduced. By the end of the war, per capita expenditures on health and education were well below pre-war levels.

Meanwhile, NGOs had begun trying to offer basic services. The government and military were very hostile to their work, since the people they were serving were considered 'the enemy'. Lack of resources and trained personnel forced NGOs to train local people as health and education workers. As the war progressed, NGOs came to play an important role in supplementing services in poor comm-unities all over the country. Despite the lack of resources, government opposition, and the NGOs' inadequate coordination and accountability to their constituents, their efforts saved many lives and provided some education for thousands of children, under extremely difficult conditions.

As the war drew to a close, statistical indicators confirmed the social crisis: only 20

right Children in an improvised classroom, on the porch of a bombed farmhouse, during the war.

Mike Goldwater/Oxfam

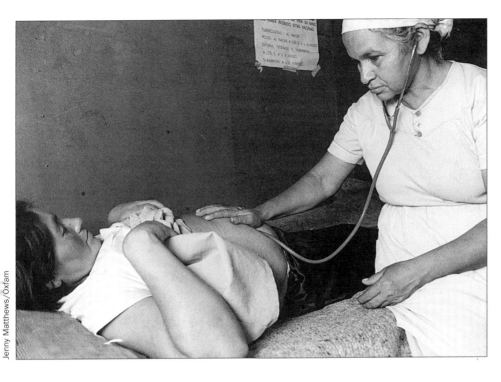

Jenny Matthews/Oxfam

left Few women in El Salvador receive an adequate level of ante-natal care.

per cent of rural population with direct access to health services; infant mortality rate at forty-six per thousand; under-five mortality, sixty per thousand, over half of these deaths due to diarrhoea, respiratory infections, and other easily-treatable diseases; a 40–1 teacher-student ratio in public schools; 15 per cent of school-aged children never attending any school; rural illiteracy rate, 35.4 per cent (55 per cent among women working in the home).[22]

After the war, poor Salvadorans were optimistic about the possibility of dramatically improving such indicators. Reconstruction funds could be used to rebuild social infrastructure in the ex-conflictive zones. Multilateral donors, especially the InterAmerican Development Bank, had noted the disastrous decline in basic services as a side-effect of structural adjustment, and were beginning to press governments to devote resources to these services.[23]

Armando Calderón Sol promised thorough reforms of the health and education systems, and pledged to increase social spending to 50 per cent of the government budget by the year 2000. Five years after the signing of the Peace Accord, the country still awaits those improve-ments. As a percentage of total public expend-iture, combined spending on health and education actually declined from 25.5 per cent in 1990 to 23.8 per cent in 1995. Increased spending on public security and debt service, as well as the maintenance of military spending levels (despite a 50 per cent cut in the armed forces) account for the slow relative growth of social spending.

Resources are only part of the problem. Bureaucracy, centralisation, and corruption pose serious obstacles to any real change.

The integration of the 'popular' educators and health promoters into ministry systems could provide a partial solution, but that integration has proven to be a slow, difficult process. One important measure of the stability of peace in El Salvador must be the extent of improvement in the everyday lives of the poor. While Angelita from Tierra Blanca had the good fortune to survive a life-threatening illness, each year thousands of other Salvadoran children are not so lucky. Similarly, glaring shortcomings in the school system leave the future uncertain for those children that survive infancy. The surge of economic growth in post-war El Salvador has resulted in precious little improvement in social services.

49

The search for an alternative

Undoubtedly, the Salvadoran economy grew impressively in the first half of the 1990s. In addition, inflation decreased, as tariffs fell, and the government imposed a value-added tax to stabilise its income. Indeed, the World Bank has referred to this period as a 'great leap forward'.[24] But growth and macroeconomic stability, however praiseworthy, do not automatically lead to long-term well-being for the majority of a country's population.

El Salvador's post-war growth spurt has depended on external resources, such as *remesas* and foreign aid, and these funds will tend to diminish as the country approaches the new millennium. While some Salvadoran exiles returned home after the war's end, the vast majority did not. Foreseeing an economic disaster if emigrants all returned, government leaders lobbied US officials to ensure at least a temporary continuation of the special immigration status accorded Salvadorans.

With a wealth of family connections abroad, and hard times at home, poor Salvadorans continue to emigrate. The official figures are notoriously unreliable, but, five years after

Chapultepec, family remittances surged past one billion dollars. (Some analysts questioned the statistics, suggesting that, by 1995, a large proportion of total inflows was related to laundered drug money.) In any case, the government acknowledges that remittances will slowly decline as Salvadorans living abroad become more integrated into their new countries. Foreign aid served as the other main external impetus for economic growth in the 1990s. The country averaged $400 million in official transfers in the period 1992-96, although that level of aid is unlikely to be maintained in future.

The 'great leap forward' has followed the pattern of exclusion typical of economic life in El Salvador since the arrival of the Spanish, with wealthy and middle-income Salvadorans benefiting disproportionately. In the first two years of the structural adjustment experiment, the share of national income going to the richest 20 per cent of Salvadoran society increased from 43.0 per cent to 54.2, while the share going to the poorest 20 per cent decreased from 5.6 per cent to 3.4 per cent. The rich are getting richer and the poor poorer at the worst possible time, just as the country tries to heal the wounds of a traumatic civil war. Current economic policies are not serving the country in its effort to construct a lasting peace, but is there an alternative?

Soon after the elections, a reporter asked new president Armando Calderón Sol about his policy on the free-enterprise zones. He replied that he did not like the idea of setting aside specific areas where foreign capital would receive privileged status: 'Why don't we turn the entire country into one big free-enterprise zone?' In 1995 the government proposed to do just that by a plan to remove all tariffs on imported goods, and tie the nation's currency to the dollar, to encourage foreign investments. In addition, structural

below Shanty town, El Salvador. Post-war growth has benefited wealthy and middle-income Salvadorans, but the poor have become poorer.

Rhodri Jones/Oxfam

adjustment was to be reinforced by privatising more state enterprises and boosting value-added tax. Where would laid-off state workers go for jobs? What about agricultural producers undermined by cheap food imports? Calderón's 'cure' might well kill the patient. Opposition from across the political spectrum, including the manufacturing and agroexport sectors making up an important part of ARENA's traditional base, caused the government to delay implementation of the proposals, but not to withdraw them.

FUNDE (the National Development Foundation), a think-tank with close ties to popular organisations and the FMLN, has set out a very different vision for the national economy, designed to produce an inclusive development process that directly addresses social, economic, and ecological issues.[25] FUNDE's tripartite plan proposes the integration of macroeconomic policy designed to produce long-term economic growth with a sectoral strategy to rebuilding the agriculture and manufacturing sectors and a social investment strategy designed to reduce poverty and transform economic growth into genuine social development.

FUNDE proposes these quite general notions as more than an economic and social blueprint; rather, as the starting point for an economic debate among all of those sectors marginalised by the government's focus on the financial and commercial sectors. FUNDE invites industrialists like those represented by ANEP (the National Association of Free Enterprise) and commercial agricultural producers to join this debate, provided that they agree that the nation's economy must be revitalised in such a way as to address the problem of mass poverty. Do such policies have any political viability in an ARENA-dominated scenario? Would the World Bank and the other international financial institutions ever agree to them? Only time can tell, but the call to such a debate can only be seen as a positive move in post-war El Salvador.

If 'new economic agents' , such as agricultural co-operatives, peasant farmers, and street vendors, are central to the alternative economic model, then a new vision must also

Rhodri Jones/Oxfam

suggest sustainable ways of including them, in the context of ecological degradation and a rapidly globalising economy. One Salvadoran development worker with long experience summed up this dilemma when he said, at the end of a long discussion of the FUNDE proposal: 'We're still missing the local part of the equation...If FUNDE was given the Ministry of Planning tomorrow, would people know what to do in San Vicente?'

In a sense, post-war El Salvador has served as a school in which thousands of poor people have set out to learn 'what to do in San Vicente' and in many other places. The conditions have been far from ideal: trying to recover psycho-logically from the war in situations of extreme poverty, and with structural adjustment erecting barrier after barrier to their efforts.

above Street-vendors on the steps outside the main market in San Salvador try to make a living by selling a few vegetables.

While it is no more than a myth that all poor people in El Salvador belong to popular organisations, poor people did inherit a high level of organisation from the war years. They have gained control of significant amounts of resources, especially land. In recent years, the organised poor have enjoyed unprecedented external resources. How have they used these resources, and what lessons have they learned?

The FUNDE prescription

In early 1996, economic indicators began to create a general perception that the economy was heading for a recession, after the rapid expansion of the early 1990s. The growth of the *maquila* sector was levelling off and the construction surge losing steam. ARENA's postwar economic model was looking shaky.

Among the policy recommendations in FUNDE's multi-faceted plan are:

- A decrease in regressive taxes like the value-added tax, with progressive taxes on income and corporate profits, and a crack-down on tax evasion.
- An emergency programme for the protection and conservation of natural resources that would promote massive reforestation, and the recognition of the country's water resources as a 'strategic natural resource'.
- Increased spending on health, education, and housing accompanied by initiatives to de-bureaucratise the public institutions responsible for these expenditures and to increase participation of beneficiaries in public programmes.
- 'Democratisation' of the credit system through the creation of new institutions and support of existing alternatives to ensure the availability of credit to small- and medium-scale producers.
- Increased public investment in social infrastructure, especially in rural areas, to create employment and improve services.
- Direct or indirect price controls on a few basic goods, such as beans, corn, sugar, cooking oil, and salt, that dominate the consumption patterns of poor Salvadorans.
- An industrial policy favouring production for the internal and regional (Central American) market.

- A self-critical appraisal of the strengths and weaknesses of public enterprises, instead of the current trend toward wholesale privatisation, and the participation of workers where privatisation does occur.

Since FUNDE has a close historical relationship to the FMLN, the similarity between the FUNDE plan and that of the Frente is not surprising. Much more noteworthy were the resemblances between the FUNDE plan and the so-called *ANEP Manifesto* published by the manufacturing and commercial interests represented in the National Free Enterprise Association (ANEP) in 1996. However, the significance of the coincidence should not be overestimated: given the historical links between ANEP and ARENA, it is unlikely that new political alliances will form on the basis of shared economic analysis. However, ARENA's economic policy was clearly being questioned, as the 1997 elections approached.

Defying even the Lempa: The SES of San Vicente

In the southern part of the department of San Vicente, 4,000 people are attempting to build a new regional economy in an area virtually abandoned during the war. In their different ways, these ex-combatants, war veterans, returned refugees, internally displaced persons, and former residents of the region have all been affected by the war.

The hardy pioneers of these new communities have faced floods, drought, bouts with cholera and malaria, hunger caused by lost harvests, and the isolation that comes with the impossibility of land transport during the long months of the rainy season. Yet they remain determined to take advantage of the opportunity to own and work their own land. Unlike other ex-conflictive zones, San Vicente has experienced a relatively trouble-free land transfer process, and most communities have achieved clear title to land.

In September 1993, at the initiative of the CORDES Foundation, a Salvadoran NGO, the communities of the zone voted to form the SES (Regional Economic System), an organisation designed, in its own words, to 'put total decision making power regarding their social and economic destiny into the hands of people who live in the sector, and to achieve a real and sustainable system of development'. CORDES set up the SES to provide productive credits to both family and collective production throughout the zone, and a multi-service centre for agricultural services such as technical assistance, fertilisers, and agricultural machinery.

At first, the communities struggled hard to survive. By 1995, however, things were improving. For Carlos Molina, of Puerto Nuevo: 'Yes, now we can begin to see the impact of the development projects, and this can only get better as the people themselves have a chance to develop their capacities.' The SES initiated an irrigation project for dry-season planting in Rancho Grande, another to bring potable water south into the zone, and a third to train residents to act as 'popular agricultural technicians' in their communities.

Formidable obstacles still faced the SES as it entered its third year of existence. Organisational and technical problems continue to limit potential increases in production. Even though the communities had gained clear title to land through the PTT, community councils did not immediately assign land to families. The resulting uncertainty made some people hesitant to fully 'buy in' to the SES model, and both family and collective production suffered. By the end of 1996, however, CORDES and the local leadership of the SES had decided to divide the land into distinct parcels based on local land-use maps, and USAID was supporting the process by providing satellite-based surveying technology.

No one can control the weather, but a system of dikes and drainage ditches controls the flooding of the Lempa River. However, the poor condition of that system presents the greatest threat to the future of the SES. USAID estimates that repairing the flood control system will cost $6 million. In September 1995, heavy rains, coupled with a decision by the electrical company to open the floodgates of a dam, caused the second devastating flood in three years.

Before the floodwater had even receded, furious SES leaders were in the Legislative Assembly demanding legislation prohibiting the electric company from opening the floodgates again without warning. With or without that legislation, in the long term the problem cries out for a financial commitment from the government to a flood-control project.

Simón Amaya, a local campesino and elected president of the SES, sees the enormity of the problem of the floods and the equally challenging social needs for adequate health care and educational services. In the long run, he says, the SES will have to confront the national government to get these needs met. For the time being, however, it will have to rely on the support of its external friends.

Recognising the hard road ahead, Simón is still optimistic: 'Yes, I do feel hopeful. The important thing is that through participating people understand more, little by little; they learn new skills, and there is advancement in the educational area. As all this happens, people begin to understand why something like the SES is important, and the project becomes more viable. Sure, today some people have their doubts, that's natural. In the future, maybe economic capacity will make it possible for us all to think differently... maybe then we won't even have to depend so much on others.'

Banking on the urban poor: PROCOMES

The 1992 census showed that, for the first time in history, the majority of the Salvadoran population lived in urban areas. The war accelerated mass urbanisation. In 1971, when the previous national census was carried out, only 39.5 per cent of a much smaller population lived in urban areas. In 20 years, the number of urban Salvadorans nearly doubled. The vast majority of the new urban population ended up in the so-called 'marginal' communities: vast, densely-populated areas often located on the periphery of the city. In San Salvador, alone, hundreds of thousands of people live in such communities, often without even the most basic amenities. Several such communities in the capital took the name 'Tenth of October' because they were formed on 10 October 1986 when a powerful earthquake devastated the city. Another huge shantytown in Soyapango is called 'Twenty-second of April', for the day when 80 families moved onto the site of an abandoned landfill. As many as 14,000 people live in a sprawling community there today.

Katalina Aneca

Katalina Aneca

During the war, community organisations emerged to help the urban poor in their struggle to legalise their claim to the land on which they lived, and to fight with municipal authorities over the provision of basic services such as water and electricity. NGOs helped communities to respond to the various emergencies that dominated everyday life.

PROCOMES (The Corporation of Communal Projects) began its work in and around San Salvador in 1988. The new conditions of peace challenged PROCOMES to reconsider its orientation toward emergency relief. 'We had to change the idea that we were working just to alleviate emergencies,' says project manager Virginia Magaña. 'We had to begin building economic and social development in the communities.'

What did this mean for communities almost totally reliant on the informal sector of the economy? For PROCOMES, it meant continuing to equip people to do battle with the authorities, but it also meant supporting them in their efforts to achieve some degree of economic security. To build that security, PROCOMES chose to use the tool of communal banks, based on the peer-lending model made famous by the Grameen Bank in Bangladesh. In 1992, PROCOMES formed its first communal bank, in the community of San Luis. A group of ten people borrowed 300 colones (£23) each from a fund provided by PROCOMES, to be paid back in four months. Besides providing the funds, PROCOMES assigns a financial advisor and trains borrowers in the use of credit, and in financial administration. Other than that, bank members are in charge: they collect debts, make decisions about new loans, and see to the overall administration of the bank.

María Antonia Ramírez, one of the original members of the San Luis Bank, sells fruit, vegetables, and drinks from a table at the front of her house. 'The money I've borrowed from the bank is a great help. Without it I wouldn't have gotten anywhere. Now I just have to see how I'm going to pay it back.' She's not worried about going into debt, though. 'If I can't sell one thing, then I'm off looking to sell something else,' she says with a proud smile.

Rina Martínez explains how the bank deals with members that fall behind in their payments. 'Everyone gets together to agree on how to respond to the case. We all take responsibility.' She emphasises, however, that such cases do not come up very often. In Rina's case, after starting out with the 300 colon loan and repaying that loan and several more, she recently borrowed 6000 colones for a much larger project. The bank has transformed her little stall into a well-stocked store with a range of goods which she can now buy at wholesale prices.

'The banks provide credit for people who would never, ever qualify for bank loans,' says Virginia from PROCOMES. 'And it gets them away from the *coyotes* in the market who are willing to lend, but at interest of up to 20 per cent per day.' The San Luis bank typically charges a rate of 3 per cent per month on its loans.

The 'Sixteenth of March' community in Soyapango set up its bank after three years of resisting the efforts of the police, and then the army, to evict them from their land. The bank is one of several community efforts led by 'the two Martas' (Marta García and Marta Hernández). Four years after its rocky beginning, the community does not yet have legal status, but it has lights and water...and it has its bank. The bank has 38 active members, 34 of them women; they have used bank loans to set up corner shops, small workshops, market stalls, and a *pupusa* stand or two. Marta Hernández, who recently borrowed 2000 colones to send her daughter to vocational school, says, 'My idea is to continue with the loans, to buy a sewing machine and try to make a little money, not a lot, not even a minimum wage, but something.'

That 90 per cent of the members in the bank are women is not at all unusual. Women head the vast majority of families in such communities. As Virginia puts it, 'We are not a women's organisation, but we recognise that our work with the banks is making us an organisation that works mostly with women. With the communities the way they are, something would be wrong with our banks if they were not mostly women.' PROCOMES has a gender programme that seeks to understand the impact of power relations between men and women in the home, on the ability of women to participate in the communal banks and other income-generating activities.

Based on three years of experience with communal banks, PROCOMES is ready to expand the programme to reach more people in more communities. Although they create significant income-producing opportunities for participants, communal banks only provide a few of the urban poor with a way out of poverty. Virginia Magaña recognises this limitation, but insists that they can not be judged on such a narrow basis. 'We in PROCOMES have an historic commitment

above Isabel Rodriguez, a founder member of the communal bank.

left Marta Hernández, one of the community leaders responsible for setting up the bank.

with people that the system has always discarded as people who don't matter. Today, maybe unlike five or ten years ago, our commitment demands that we try to do something to help people build some basic economic capacity and stability. With all their limitations, the communal banks have done this in many cases, and until we find a better way to respond to poverty in the communities we will help people form banks. The people are happy with our decision, and that is very important to us.'

Co-operatives take a big step forward: SOCRA

As the kingpin of the agroexport economy for over a century, coffee, the 'golden bean', established itself as the archetypal symbol of economic injustice in El Salvador. While coffee cultivation made huge fortunes for a few families, it provided only the barest subsistence for hundreds of thousands of Salvadorans, including seasonal coffee workers and small-scale cultivators. The 1980 agrarian reform distributed dozens of the largest coffee estates to co-operatives made up primarily of workers on those estates. But the highly profitable activities of processing and exporting coffee remained in the hands of the old oligarchy.

In the mid-1980s, co-operative leaders, including René Hernández, began to devise a way in which small co-operatives would be able to regain the 30–50 per cent of the value of their coffee that they lost after harvesting. 'We wanted to build a new *beneficio* [processing plant], obtain an export license, and market our coffee without the big private people ever seeing it.'

Through war and peace, René and his co-workers doggedly pursued their dream against apparently impossible odds. Eventually, in October 1994, they inaugurated a new, state-of-the-art coffee *beneficio* near the Pan-American highway in the department of Santa Ana, the country's richest coffee region. 'You wouldn't believe how many times people told me that we were crazy to think we could do it...especially when coffee prices dropped so quickly. On many occasions, I thought we were crazy, too, but other *compañeros* encouraged us to keep going. I don't know if we could have done it without our friends in the international

agencies.' The $800,000 credit for the construction of the *beneficio* came from a European development finance agency, EDCS (Ecumenical Development Council Service), whose investment was guaranteed by a Belgian bank brought into the process by Oxfam Belgium.

A year earlier, fifteen coffee co-operatives had formed SOCRA (the Society of Agrarian Reform Co-operatives) the company that owns the *beneficio* and the hard-won licence to export coffee. In 1993, SOCRA did a trial run, processing coffee in a nearby co-operative-owned plant and then exporting in its own name. For once, the gods of the international market co-operated with a grassroots venture, and the price of coffee surged upward just as the SOCRA coffee hit the market.

The people in the SOCRA co-operatives feel positive about the benefits. For Ricardo Antonio Martínez, founding member of San Antonio Zacamil co-operative: 'For me, it's been great. When we've needed the help of SOCRA, they have responded. Sometimes a farmer can't work for lack of money...SOCRA provided money when we most needed it. We can really talk with them, about our work and other things, talk that could never happen in the private *beneficios*.' Andrés de Jesus Caledonia, also of San Antonio Zacamil, explains: 'SOCRA gives us the opportunity to learn lots of things. How this sack of coffee is processed, and how it gets to the market in Europe and the US. Our participation has had benefits for both SOCRA and our co-operative.'

As well as processing and exporting coffee, SOCRA employs technicians that travel regularly to the co-operatives, helping them to resolve production problems. However, the co-operatives will only work with SOCRA if it makes economic sense to do so. One indicator of the viability of SOCRA is the price it pays for the coffee, and SOCRA has already proved to be very competitive in this respect. The credit needs expressed by Ricardo pose a more difficult dilemma. SOCRA must be able to extend credit to the cash-starved co-ops against their harvest in order for them to be able to participate. Otherwise, SOCRA will have no coffee to process in its shiny, new plant.

The project began with small credits from international agencies. They also borrowed $20,000 from a bank, using their office building as collateral, but now SOCRA faces a credit squeeze. These credits enabled SOCRA to survive the first year, but, as they prepared for the next harvest, the co-operatives needed further credit. After overcoming the barriers of control of the processing and export of their product, SOCRA now faced the stone wall of the Salvadoran banking system. In response to the emergency, the international organisations all expanded their credit commitments, but they cannot substitute indefinitely for a supportive banking system.

Undaunted, SOCRA is pressing forward and hoping to expand to other areas of the country. News of their experiences has spread around the small world of Salvadoran coffee co-operatives, and 12 more co-operatives are in the process of affiliating. With the modesty that comes from not knowing what will happen tomorrow, René Hernández assesses SOCRA's success: 'Obviously having a *beneficio* is an excellent achievement, but now we have to move enough coffee to be able to pay salaries and interest, and to extend credits. Without that, we won't benefit anyone. But, still, to go from being a *pinche campesino*, as they call us, that only knew how to go out and bake in the sun, to being able to run an enterprise like this one is also an achievement....'

The SES, PROCOMES and SOCRA represent three different attempts to create economic opportunities for specific groups of poor Salvadorans. Other groups of ex-refugees, ex-combatants, co-operative members, and urban women are engaged in similar experiments all over the country. To their credit, the

same international NGOs that helped these groups to survive during the war have continued to support them as they face the new challenges of peace. Although such attempts at self-reliance are tiny in relation to the huge problems of poverty in El Salvador, they provide examples of alternatives to structural adjustment which could be more widely replicated.

Salvadoran NGOs: the challenge of change

In the course of the war, the Salvadoran NGO sector grew from a handful of charity clubs into a varied collection of hundreds of organisations providing a wide range of services. As in so many other areas of social life during the war years, El Salvador's churches played a critical role in this development. In the early 1980s, with almost all avenues of social action closed off by repression, church workers took tremendous risks in establishing NGOs, and many dedicated individuals paid with their lives for the privilege of providing relief to tens of thousands of internally displaced people.

Almost all NGOs had close links to either the FMLN's revolutionary project or the counterinsurgency strategy advanced by the government. The civil war influenced everything they did, including the day-to-day choices of where and how to work. The complex political situation created formidable barriers to NGO coordination; several organisations in the same area provided identical services to people differentiated only by their particular party connections within the FMLN.

While peace made it possible to work more openly on long-term development, NGOs needed new personnel and administrative procedures as well as fresh strategic orientations. Rapid institutional change (called *reconversion* by the Salvadorans) engulfed all local NGOs in the mid-1990s, as political alliances were re-examined, and vertical wartime structures were changed to give constituents more control over the organisations designed to serve them.

above, top SOCRA meeting, where everyone can say what they think should be done and decisions are made democratically.

above The processing plant provides employment for local people, and ensures that growers earn more from the coffee they produce.

Opportunity in danger

Ivan Montecinos

On October 31, 1995, President Armando Calderón Sol brought 'good news' to the Salvadoran people: that the implementation of the Peace Accord was now officially over. According to the president, 95 per cent of the Accord had been fulfilled, and the other 5 per cent had been rescheduled for completion in the next few months. For Calderón Sol, 'this official announcement is not only good news for the Salvadoran people, but also grounds for legitimate pride, since peace is a victory and an asset which we have all achieved with great effort and sacrifice.' However, other problems such as the alarming national crime wave and continuing economic deprivation had long since replaced compliance with the Peace Accord as the primary concern of most Salvadorans.

Always a problem in El Salvador, crime exploded after the end of the war. By the mid-1990s, the murder rate in San Salvador was higher than that in crime-ridden US cities such as Los Angeles or Miami. A survey found that just under 60 per cent of Salvadorans reported that they or a member of their family had been a victim of a violent crime; half of all respondents identified crime

above Union member and his small daughter at the celebration of the Peace Accords, 16 January 1992.

as the country's worst problem, with 'economic insecurity' a poor second at 17 per cent. Kidnapping for ransom had become commonplace.

Despite wide public awareness that organised crime involved people close to the military and the ARENA party, the government chose not to pursue those links but instead, called the army out to police the streets and passed emergency legislation that threatened the fragile efforts to reform the notoriously corrupt justice system. Then, in 1996, despite strong opposition and doubts about its efficacy in fighting crime, ARENA took steps to reintroduce the death penalty.

Official intolerance of opposition was demonstrated in various ways. Citing violations of law, the government shut down a dozen community radios that had served as important sources of free expression in the country's ex-conflictive zones. After a long battle, ARENA pushed through the National Assembly a bill giving the Ministry of the Interior significant control over the activities of NGOs. As the Salvadoran economy faltered, it was clear that economic growth had not resulted in an improvement in living conditions for poor Salvadorans. Street demonstrations by war veterans and other social groups grew in militancy, and the government responded with increasing violence. The Salvadoran people repudiated such policies and practices by voting for the FMLN and other opposition parties in 1997.

The Chapultepec Accord represented a series of accommodations made by all sectors of society to respond to the overwhelming desire of the Salvadoran people for an end to the conflict. Those accommodations included a number of democratic reforms and new institutions that provided an opportunity for the country to escape from its authoritarian past. If the reforms contained in the Peace Accord are not successfully consolidated and broadened to include a democratisation of control over the country's resources, then peace will not fulfil its promise. In the absence of openness to opposition and policies that directly address the persistence of mass poverty, the resentments created by inequality and intolerance will produce shock waves that will shatter the fragile democracy struggling to survive in Latin America's 'little finger.' After a confrontation with police in late 1995, one war veteran remarked that, 'In this country it is harder to get rice and beans than weapons to begin a new war.' If he is right, democracy is in trouble whether or not a new war is on the horizon.

The 1997 elections, which increased the number of opposition members in the legislative assembly, and the number of municipalities controlled by the FMLN and its allies, gave grounds for hope that democracy is alive and well in El Salvador, and that the Chapultepec Accords have changed things for the better. However, it remains to be seen if the new balance of political power will bring action to address the problems of poverty and crime.

Five years after the end of a civil war of unprecedented ferocity, El Salvador remains at the threshold of a door to a new future opened by peace. Many Salvadorans, including people featured in this book, such as Miriam Chicas, Vilma Sanchez, Simón Amaya, and Santiago, have been attempting to move their country forward, through that door; but economic injustice weighs heavily against them. Without freeing themselves of that weight, they could not take full advantage of the opportunities of peace. Unfortunately, the door opened by peace will not stay open forever. If El Salvador can not take forward this opportunity for change, when will another one appear?

Notes

1 For excerpts of Alvarado's account, see Roque Dalton, *Las Historias Prohibidas del Pulgarcito* (San Salvador: UCA Editores, 1988), pp. 9–17.

2 The story of *La Matanza* is told in great detail in Thomas P. Anderson, *Matanza: El Salvador's Communist Revolt* (Lincoln: University of Nebraska Press, 1971).

3 William Durham, *Scarcity and Survival in Central America: The Ecological Origins of the Soccer War* (Palo Alto: Stanford University Press, 1979), p. 48.

4 For a moving collection of first person stories of the popular church in El Salvador, see Scott Wright, *A Spring Whose Waters Never Run Dry* (Washington, DC: EPICA, 1990).

5 Among the best treatments of the remarkable life of Monseñor Romero, are James R. Brockman, *Romero: A Life* (Maryknoll, NY: Orbis Books, 1989) or María López Vigil, *Piezas Para un Retrato* (San Salvador: UCA Editores, 1993).

6 This figure is very difficult to confirm because of the large amount of covert aid for which there has never been a proper accounting. See Benjamin Schwarz, *American Counterinsurgency Doctrine and El Salvador: the Frustrations of Reform and the Illusions of Nation Building* (Washington, DC: The Rand Corporation, 1992), p.2.

7 Testimony taken from *Project Salvador Update* (translation by Patty Lawless), October 1996, pp 1–2.

8 Teresa Whitfield, *Paying the Price: Ignacio Ellacuría and the Murdered Jesuits of El Salvador* (Philadelphia: Temple University Press, 1994), Chapter 10.

9 IDESES/CRIES, *Proceso de paz en El Salvador: La solución política negociada* (Managua & San Salvador: CRIES, 1992).

10 For a good summation of the content of the peace accord, see Jack Spence, et. al., *A Negotiated Revolution? A Two Year Progress Report on the Salvadoran Peace Accords* (Cambridge, MA: Hemisphere Initiatives, 1994).

11 Interview with Anders Kompass, then Director of UNDP office in San Salvador, March 1994.

12 Doug Farah, "Salvadorans Still Up in Arms Over Land Reform", *The Washington Post*, November 21, 1995, p. A12.

13 See Mitchell Seligson, et. al., *El Salvador Agricultural Policy Analysis Land Tenure Study*, (USAID Contracts Nos. DAN-4084-z-11-8034-00 and LAG-4084-C-00-2043-00), September 1993.

14 See Kevin Murray, et.al., *Rescuing Reconstruction: The Debate on Postwar Economic Recovery in El Salvador* (Cambridge, MA: Hemisphere Initiatives), 1994.

15 CIDAI, "Maquila Troubles," *Proceso*, November 6, 1996, p. 4 (English translation by publisher).

16 Alvaro de Soto & Graciela de Castillo, "Obstacles to Peacebuilding," *Foreign Policy*, Vol. 94 (Spring), pp.69–83.

17 For an in-depth analysis of this contradiction, see James K. Boyce (ed.), *Economic Policy for Building Peace: The Lessons of El Salvador* (Boulder: Lynne Reiner, 1996).

18 See, for example, USECOM, *Free and Fair: The Conduct of El Salvador's 1994 Elections* (Washington, DC: USECOM, 1994).

19 United Nations, *De La Locura a la Esperanza: La Guerra de 12 Años en El Salvador* (New York & San Salvador: United Nations, 1993), p. 132.

20 Quoted in, "Gender in Focus: Adjusting Development Strategies for Gender," *El Salvador Information Project*, San Salvador, September 1994.

21 For a complete discussion of the twisted tale of Finca El Espino, see Andrew Wheat, "El Salvador's Land Deform," *Multinational Monitor*, September 1996, pp. 16–19.

22 Sources include the *UN Human Development Report* for 1995, *Estudios Centroamericanos* for May-June 1994, and the Salvadoran government's *1994 Multi-Purpose Household Survey*.

23 See the collected proceedings of a 1993 conference on just this theme in *Reforma Social y Pobreza* (New York: InterAmerican Development Bank and United Nations Development Programme, 1993).

24 *El Salvador: Meeting the Challenge of Globalization*, (Washington, DC: The World Bank, 1996), *p. xiii*.

25 Roberto Rubio Fabian, et. al., *Crecimiento estéril o desarrollo?* (San Salvador: Equipo Maíz, 1996).

Oxfam in El Salvador

Oxfam began working in El Salvador in 1970. Oxfam has always worked through communities, popular organisations, churches and NGOs, supporting and providing solidarity to the victims of the conflict and the poor.

Community organisations supported by Oxfam are helping people to acquire the technical and organisational skills which will give them

Jenny Matthews /Oxfam

a secure livelihood. Reconciliation at community level and nationwide is giving people the confidence to build a more hopeful future – putting the old distrust and insecurity behind them.

Oxfam is funding reconstruction and rehabilitation projects in former war zones. In San Vicente, an area of heavy fighting which was abandoned during the war, Oxfam supports people who have returned to their communities in developing agricultural production and co-operatives. They have helped to establish community credit schemes and offer technical advice to small farmers, trying to encourage new ventures like fruit and dairy production in addition to corn. Oxfam also supports small coffee producers in their efforts to break through the monopolies and find new markets for their coffee in Europe and North America.

Oxfam funds women's projects, carrying out training and education programmes with women in former war zones, providing leadership training in communities which were affected by the war, to enable them to get together and lobby for their basic rights and those of their communities. With Oxfam's help, women are talking to local government authorities, and demanding services for their communities.

Urban poverty has reached dramatic levels and an increasing number of shanty town communities are ignored by mainstream government programmes. Oxfam supports organisations providing legal and technical assistance and training with the aim of helping these communities find self-sufficient ways of making a living. Oxfam also supports credit programmes for small-scale loans through communal banks. The credit is combined with training and technical help in business administration, basic financial administration and accounting.

Facts
and Figures

Land area: 20,720 sq. km.

Population: 5.94 million (1995)

Population growth rate: 3.3% p.a. (1990-94)

Urban population as percentage of total: 45%

Urban population average growth rate:
2.8% p.a. (1960-93)

Average number of children born per woman:
4 (1992)

Maternal mortality: 300 per 100,000 births

Infant mortality: 42 per 1,000 live births

Under-5 mortality: 56 per 1,000 live births

Percentage of children under 5 malnourished:
22% (1989-95 average)

Average life-expectancy: 67 (UK 76)

Adult literacy: 70% (72% men, 68% women)

GNP per capita: 1,320$

External debt: 2,770 $M

Average economic growth 1985–94:
2.2% p.a.

Public expenditure, as percentage of GNP:
military 1.7%;
education 1.8%;
health services 2.6%

One doctor for every 1,563 people

**Percentage of population with access to
health services:** 40%; **to safe water:** 55%;
to sanitation: 81%

Principal exports: *maquila* goods: 764.9$M;
coffee: 339 $M

Main trading partner:
53% of total exports to USA

Sources: Economic Intelligence Unit
Country Profile and Country Report;
UNDP, Human Development Report 1996;
World Bank World Development Report 1996.

Acknowledgements

I am greatly indebted to Mike Larrchin, who provided interviews, background material, and analysis, and who edited and commented on early drafts of the text. His understanding of the country and its people was of immense help to me in writing this book.

While I can not hope to mention all of the dozens of people who lent their support to this project, I would be particularly remiss if I did not recognise Ellen Coletti, who not only edited the text several times, but provided an indispensable reality check throughout. Mark Smith wrote the original story about his neighbour, Santiago, and Jack Spence reviewed the entire text, avoiding many hideous factual errors. Simon, Yanci, Galio, Pati, and Arely at the Oxfam office in San Salvador opened their work to my prying eyes and guided me in the most helpful way possible. As usual, the responsiblity for all errors and shortcomings is mine.

Kevin Murray, June 1997

Sources and further reading

Manilo Argueta, *One Day of Life* (New York, NY: Vintage Books, 1981).

Leigh Binford, *The El Mozote Massacre* (Tuscon, AZ: University of Arizona Press, 1996).

James K Boyce (ed.), *Economic Policies for Building Peace: The Lessons of El Salvador* (Boulder, CO: Lynne Reinner Publishers, 1996).

Beth Cagan and Steven Cagan, *This Promised Land, El Salvador: The Refugee Community of Colomoncagua and Their Return to Morazán* (New Brunswick, NJ: Rutgers University Press, 1991).

Roque Dalton (edited by Hardie St. Martin), *Small Hours of the Night* (Willimantic, CT: Curbstone Press, 1996).

Tommie Sue Montgomery, *Revolution in El Salvador: from Civil Strife to Civil Peace* (Boulder, CO: Westview Press, 1995).

Kevin Murray, *Inside El Salvador* (Albuquerque, NM: The Resource Center, 1995).

Minor Sinclair, (ed.), *The New Politics of Survival: Grassroots Movements in Central America* (New York, NY: Monthly Review Press, 1995).

Jack Spence, et. al., *Chapultepec: Five Years Later: El Salvador's Political Reality and Uncertain Future* (Cambridge, MA: Hemisphere Initiatives, 1997).

William Stanley, *The Protection Racket State: Elite Politics, Military Extortion, and Civil War in El Salvador* (Philadelphia, PA: Temple University Press, 1996).

United Nations, *The United Nations and El Salvador 1990–95* (New York: UN Blue Book Series).

Teresa Whitfield, *Paying the Price: Ignacio Ellacuría and the Murdered Jesuits of El Salvador* (Philadelphia, PA: Temple University Press, 1995).

Anjali Sundaram and George Gelber, (eds.), *A Decade of War* (New York: Monthly Review Press, 1995).

Published by Oxfam (UK and Ireland), 274 Banbury Road, Oxford OX2 7DZ, UK (registered as a charity, no. 202918)

Available in Ireland from Oxfam in Ireland, 19 Clanwilliam Terrace, Dublin 2 (tel. 01 661 8544).

OX413/RB/97
Printed by Oxfam Print Unit

Oxfam (UK and Ireland) is a member of Oxfam International.

Oxfam (United Kingdom and Ireland) publishes a wide range of books, manuals, and resource materials for specialist, academic, and general readers. For a free catalogue, please write to:

Oxfam Publishing
274 Banbury Road
Oxford OX2 7DZ, UK

telephone: 01865 313922
fax: 01865 313925
e-mail: publish@oxfam.org.uk

If you wish to comment on any aspect of Oxfam publications, please write to the editorial team at Oxfam Publications, at the above address.